The Dream of the
Unified Field

Jorie Graham

THE DREAM OF THE
UNIFIED FIELD

Selected Poems 1974–1994

ecco

An Imprint of HarperCollins Publishers

Printed in the United States of America. No part of this book may be used or
reproduced in any manner whatsoever without written permission except in
the case of brief quotations embodied in critical articles and reviews. For
information address HarperCollins Publishers,
195 Broadway, New York, NY 10007.

HarperCollins books may be purchased for educational, business, or sales
promotional use. For information, please e-mail the Special Markets Depart-
ment at SPsales@harpercollins.com.

First Ecco edition 2002

Library of Congress Cataloging-in-Publication Data

Graham, Jorie, 1950–
The dream of the unified field : selected poems, 1974–1994
p. cm.
ISBN 0-88001-438-5
0-88001-476-8 (paperback)
I. Title.
PS3557.R214D73   1995
811'.54—dc20   95-16572

The text of this book is set in Bembo
Text design by Richard Oriolo

24 25 26 27 28 LBC 29 28 27 26 25

CONTENTS

from MATERIALISM

from

HYBRIDS OF PLANTS
AND OF GHOSTS

THE WAY THINGS WORK

is by admitting
or opening away.
This is the simplest form
of current: Blue
moving through blue;
blue through purple;
the objects of desire
opening upon themselves
without us;
the objects of faith.
The way things work
is by solution,
resistance lessened or
increased and taken
advantage of.
The way things work
is that we finally believe
they are there,
common and able
to illustrate themselves.
Wheel, kinetic flow,
rising and falling water,
ingots, levers and keys,
I believe in you,
cylinder lock, pully,
lifting tackle and
crane lift your small head—
I believe in you—
your head is the horizon to
my hand. I believe
forever in the hooks.
The way things work
is that eventually
something catches.

HYBRIDS OF PLANTS
AND OF GHOSTS

I understand that it is grafting,
this partnership of lost wills, common flowers.

That only perfection can be kept, not
its perfect instances. Snap-

dragon what can I expect of you,
dress of the occasion?

So I am camouflaged,
so the handsome bones make me invisible.

It is useless. Randomness,
the one lost handkerchief at my heart,

is the one I dropped and know
to look for. Indeed, clues,

how partial I am to bleeding hues,
to clustering. Almond,

stone fruit,
you would be a peach, an apricot—

but see how close you can come without
already being there, the evening pulled in

at your waist, slipping over your feet,
driving them firmly into place,

the warm evening saying Step, anywhere you go
is yours, sweet scent in a hurry, to bloom is to be

taken completely—.
White petals, creaseless and ambitious,

may I break your even weave, loosen your knot,

and if I break you are you mine?

I WAS TAUGHT THREE

names for the tree facing my window
almost within reach, elastic

with squirrels, memory banks, homes.
Castagno took itself to heart, its pods

like urchins clung to where they landed
claiming every bit of shadow

at the hem. *Chassagne*, on windier days,
nervous in taffeta gowns,

whispering, on the verge of being
anarchic, though well bred.

And then *chestnut*, whipped pale and clean
by all the inner reservoirs

called upon to do their even share of work.
It was not the kind of tree

got at by default—imagine that—not one
in which only the remaining leaf

was loyal. No, this
was all first person, and I

was the stem, holding within myself the whole
bouquet of three,

at once given and received: smallest roadmaps
of coincidence. What is the idea

that governs blossoming? The human tree
clothed with its nouns, or this one

just outside my window promising more firmly
than can be

that it will reach my sill eventually, the leaves
silent as suppressed desires, and I

a name among them.

TENNESSEE JUNE

This is the heat that seeks the flaw in everything
and loves the flaw.
Nothing is heavier than its spirit,
nothing more landlocked than the body within it.
Its daylilies grow overnight, our lawns
bare, then falsely gay, then bare again. Imagine
your mind wandering without its logic,
your body the sides of a riverbed giving in . . .
In it, no world can survive
having more than its neighbors;
in it, the pressure to become forever less is the pressure
to take forevermore
to get there. Oh

let it touch you . . .
The porch is sharply lit—little box of the body—
and the hammock swings out easily over its edge.
Beyond, the hot ferns bed, and fireflies gauze
the fat tobacco slums,
the crickets boring holes into the heat the crickets fill.
Rock out into that dark and back to where
the blind moths circle, circle,
back and forth from the bone-white house to the creepers unbraiding.
Nothing will catch you.
Nothing will let you go.
We call it blossoming—
the spirit breaks from you and you remain.

JACKPOT

Halfway through Illinois on the radio
they are giving away jackpots.
I can hear them squeal as they win.
Luck in this landscape lies flat
as if to enter the ground and add to it as well.
You can see its traces, milkweed caught in the fences,
the sheen on the new grass
that could be sunshine or white paint.
But the brushstroke is visible.
We wouldn't believe anything we saw without it—

the brown, the green, the rectangle, the overpass.
I believe now that sorrow
is our presence in this by default.
In a little while I hope there will be shadows,
the houses and these trees trying to bury half of themselves.
This could be your lucky day,
the day the roof is put on the house,
and the willows once again resemble trees,
and the bridge falls in, making the river once again
sufficiently hard to cross.

ONE IN THE HAND

A bird re-entering a bush,
like an idea regaining
its intention, seeks
the missed discoveries
before attempting
flight again.
The small black spirit
tucks in its wings,
softest accordion
whose music is
the perfect landing,
the disappearance
into the dangerous
wintered body
of forsythia. Just as
from time to time
we need to seize again
the whole language
in search of
better desires.
If we could only imagine
a better arc
of flight; you get
just what you want.
And see how beautiful
an alphabet becomes
when randomness sets in,
like mother tired
after disappointment,
and keeping us
uninformed—the man
walking away whom we
want to recall
and in whom we invest

the whole explanation.
One in the hand,
one in the mind,
how clearly you know
what you have, how clearly
what he'll want to do, and do
when you let go.

THE GEESE

Today as I hang out the wash I see them again, a code
as urgent as elegant,
tapering with goals.
For days they have been crossing. We live beneath these geese

as if beneath the passage of time, or a most perfect heading.
Sometimes I fear their relevance.
Closest at hand,
between the lines,

the spiders imitate the paths the geese won't stray from,
imitate them endlessly to no avail:
things will not remain connected,
will not heal,

and the world thickens with texture instead of history,
texture instead of place.
Yet the small fear of the spiders
binds and binds

the pins to the lines, the lines to the eaves, to the pincushion bush,
as if, at any time, things could fall further apart
and nothing could help them
recover their meaning. And if these spiders had their way,

chainlink over the visible world,
would we be in or out? I turn to go back in.
There is a feeling the body gives the mind
of having missed something, a bedrock poverty, like falling

without the sense that you are passing through one world,
that you could reach another
anytime. Instead the real
is crossing you,

your body an arrival
you know is false but can't outrun. And somewhere in between
these geese forever entering and
these spiders turning back,

this astonishing delay, the everyday, takes place.

MIND

The slow overture of rain,
each drop breaking
without breaking into
the next, describes
the unrelenting, syncopated
mind. Not unlike
the hummingbirds
imagining their wings
to be their heart, and swallows
believing the horizon
to be a line they lift
and drop. What is it
they cast for? The poplars,
advancing or retreating,
lose their stature
equally, and yet stand firm,
making arrangements
in order to become
imaginary. The city
draws the mind in streets,
and streets compel it
from their intersections
where a little
belongs to no one. It is
what is driven through
all stationary portions
of the world, gravity's
stake in things. The leaves,
pressed against the dank
window of November
soil, remain unwelcome
till transformed, parts
of a puzzle unsolvable
till the edges give a bit

and soften. See how
then the picture becomes clear,
the mind entering the ground
more easily in pieces,
and all the richer for it.

OVER AND OVER STITCH

Late in the season the world digs in, the fat blossoms
hold still for just a moment longer.
Nothing looks satisfied,
but there is no real reason to move on much further:
this isn't a bad place;
why not pretend

we wished for it?
The bushes have learned to live with their haunches.
The hydrangea is resigned
to its pale and inconclusive utterances.
Towards the end of the season
it is not bad

to have the body. To have experienced joy
as the mere lifting of hunger
is not to have known it
less. The tobacco leaves
don't mind being removed
to the long racks—all uses are astounding

to the used.
There are moments in our lives which, threaded, give us heaven—
noon, for instance, or all the single victories
of gravity, or the kudzu vine,
most delicate of manias,
which has pressed its luck

this far this season.
It shines a gloating green.
Its edges darken with impatience, a kind of wind.
Nothing again will ever be this easy, lives
being snatched up like dropped stitches, the dry stalks of daylilies
marking a stillness we can't keep.

A FEATHER FOR VOLTAIRE

The bird is an alphabet, it flies
above us, catch
as catch can,
a flock,
a travel plan.
Some never touch ground.

And each flight is an arc to buttress the sky,
a loan to the sky.
And the little words we make of them, the single feathers, dropped
for us to recover,
fall and fall,
a nimble armor . . .

Feather feather of this morning where does your garden grow
flying upwind, saying look
it is safe
never to land,
it is better.
A man full of words

is a garden of weeds,
and when the weeds grow,
a garden of snow,
a necklace of tracks: it was here, my snow owl perhaps.
Who scared it away?
I, said the sparrow,

with my need, its arrow. And so here I belong, trespassing, alone,
in this nation of turns
not meant to be taken
I've taken.
A feather,
pulled from the body or found on the snow

can be dipped into ink
to make one or more words: *possessive, the sun.* A pen
can get drunk,
having come so far, having so far to go—*meadow,*
in vain, imagine
the pain

and when he was gone then there was none

and this is the key to the kingdom.

from

EROSION

SAN SEPOLCRO

In this blue light
    I can take you there,
snow having made me
    a world of bone
seen through to. This
    is my house,

my section of Etruscan
    wall, my neighbor's
lemontrees, and, just below
    the lower church,
the airplane factory.
    A rooster

crows all day from mist
    outside the walls.
There's milk on the air,
    ice on the oily
lemonskins. How clean
    the mind is,

holy grave. It is this girl
    by Piero
della Francesca, unbuttoning
    her blue dress,
her mantle of weather,
    to go into

labor. Come, we can go in.
    It is before
the birth of god. No one
    has risen yet
to the museums, to the assembly
    line—bodies

and wings—to the open air
    market. This is
what the living do: go in.
    It's a long way.
And the dress keeps opening
    from eternity

to privacy, quickening.
    Inside, at the heart,
is tragedy, the present moment
    forever stillborn,
but going in, each breath
    is a button

coming undone, something terribly
    nimble-fingered
finding all of the stops.

READING PLATO

This is the story
    of a beautiful
lie, what slips
    through my fingers,
your fingers. It's winter,
    it's far

in the lifespan
    of man.
Bareheaded, in a soiled
    shirt,
speechless, my friend
    is making

lures, his hobby. Flies
    so small
he works with tweezers and
    a magnifying glass.
They must be
    so believable

they're true—feelers,
    antennae,
quick and frantic
    as something
drowning. His heart
    beats wildly

in his hands. It is
    blinding
and who will forgive him
    in his tiny
garden? He makes them
    out of hair,

deer hair, because it's hollow
    and floats.
Past death, past sight,
    this is
his good idea, what drives
    the silly days

together. Better than memory. Better
    than love.
Then they are done, a hook
    under each pair
of wings, and it's Spring,
    and the men

wade out into the riverbed
    at dawn. Above,
the stars still connect-up
    their hungry animals.
Soon they'll be satisfied
    and go. Meanwhile

upriver, downriver, imagine, quick
    in the air,
in flesh, in a blue
    swarm of
flies, our knowledge of
    the graceful

deer skips easily across
    the surface.
Dismembered, remembered,
    it's finally
alive. Imagine
    the body

they were all once
    a part of,
these men along the lush
    green banks
trying to slip in
    and pass

for the natural world.

SCIROCCO

In Rome, at 26
 Piazza di Spagna,
at the foot of a long
 flight of
stairs, are rooms
 let to Keats

in 1820,
 where he died. Now
you can visit them,
 the tiny terrace,
the bedroom. The scraps
 of paper

on which he wrote
 lines
are kept behind glass,
 some yellowing,
some xeroxed or
 mimeographed. . . .

Outside his window
 you can hear the scirocco
working
 the invisible.
Every dry leaf of ivy
 is fingered,

refingered. Who is
 the nervous spirit
of this world
 that must go over and over
what it already knows,
 what is it

so hot and dry
     that's looking through us,
by us,
     for its answer?
In the arbor
     on the terrace

the stark hellenic
     forms
of grapes have appeared.
     They'll soften
till weak enough
     to enter

our world, translating
     helplessly
from the beautiful
     to the true. . . .
Whatever the spirit,
     the thickening grapes

are part of its looking,
     and the slow hands
that made this mask
     of Keats
in his other life,
     and the old woman,

the memorial's
     custodian,
sitting on the porch
     beneath the arbor
sorting chick-peas
     from pebbles

into her cast-iron
        pot.
See what her hands
        know—
they are its breath,
        its mother

tongue, dividing,
        discarding.
There is light playing
        over the leaves,
over her face,
        making her

abstract, making
        her quick
and strange. But she
        has no care
for what speckles her,
        changing her,

she is at
        her work. Oh how we want
to be taken
        and changed,
want to be mended
        by what we enter.

Is it thus
        with the world?
Does it wish us
        to mend it,
light and dark,
        green

and flesh? Will it
        be free then?
I think the world
        is a desperate
element. It would have us
        calm it,

receive it. Therefore this
        is what I
must ask you
        to imagine: wind;
the moment
        when the wind

drops; and grapes,
        which are nothing,
which break
        in your hands.

THE AGE OF REASON

1

The anxious bird in the wild
    spring green
is *anting,* which means,
    in my orchard
he has opened his wings
    over a furious

anthill and will take up
    into the delicate
ridges of quince-yellow
    feathers
a number of tiny, angry
    creatures

that will inhabit him, bewildered
    no doubt,
traveling deep
    into the air
on this feathery planet,
    new life. . . .

We don't know why
    they do it.
At times they'll take on
    almost anything
that burns, spreading
    their wings

over coals, over cigarette
    butts,
even, mistakenly, on bits

of broken glass.
Meanwhile the light keeps
     stroking them

as if it were love. The garden
     continues its work
all round them, the gradual
     openings that stand
for death. Under the plastic
     groundcover the human

garden grows: help-sticks
     and knots, row
after row. Who wouldn't want
     to take
into the self
     something that burns

or cuts, or wanders
     lost
over the body?

2

At the end of Werner Herzog's
     Woyzeck,
after the hero whom
     we love
who is mad has
     murdered

the world, the young
     woman
who is his wife,
     and loved her,
and covered himself
     with blood,

he grows frightened
        by how quickly
she softens and takes on the shape
        of the soil.
In the moonlight he throws
        his knife

into the wide river
        flowing beside them
but doesn't think it has
        reached deep
enough so goes in
        after it

himself. White as a knife,
        he goes in after it
completely. The trees are green.
        The earth
is green. The light
        is sick

with green. Now that
        he's gone
the woman is a tiny
        gap
in green. Next day,
        in slow

motion, the undertakers and
        philosophers
(it is the Age of
        Reason)
wander through the tall
        and glossy

ferns and grasses
        looking for

the instrument. It's spring.
　　The air is
gold. Every now and then
　　they lift

the white sheet they have
　　laid to see
what death is. They are
　　meticulous,
the day is everything
　　they have.

　　　　　3

How far is true
　　enough?
How far into the
　　earth
can vision go and
　　still be

love? Isn't the
　　honesty
of things where they
　　resist,
where only the wind
　　can bend them

back, the real weather,
　　not our
desire hissing Tell me
　　your parts
that I may understand
　　your body,

your story. Which is why

we have
characters and the knife
    of a plot
to wade through this
    current. Now

it's blossoms
    back to back
through the orchard.
    A surf
of tenderness. There is
    no deep

enough. For what we want
    to take
inside of us, whole orchard,
    color,
name, scent, symbol, raw
    pale

blossoms, wet black
    arms there is
no deep enough.

34

WANTING A CHILD

How hard it is for the river here to re-enter
the sea, though it's most beautiful, of course, in the waste
of time where it's almost
turned back. Then
it's yoked,
trussed. . . . The river
has been everywhere, imagine, dividing, discerning,
cutting deep into the parent rock,
scouring and scouring
its own bed.
Nothing is whole
where it has been. Nothing
remains unsaid.
Sometimes I'll come this far from home
merely to dip my fingers in this glittering, archaic
sea that renders everything
identical, flesh
where mind and body
blur. The seagulls squeak, ill-fitting
hinges, the beach is thick
with shells. The tide
is always pulsing upward, inland, into the river's rapid
argument, pushing
with its insistent tragic waves—the living echo,
says my book, of some great storm far out at sea, too far
to be recalled by us
but transferred
whole onto this shore by waves, so that erosion
is its very face.

I WATCHED A SNAKE

hard at work in the dry grass
    behind the house
catching flies. It kept on
    disappearing.
And though I know this has
    something to do

with lust, today it seemed
    to have to do
with work. It took it almost half
    an hour to thread
roughly ten feet of lawn,
    so slow

between the blades you couldn't see
    it move. I'd watch
its path of body in the grass go
    suddenly invisible
only to reappear a little
    further on

black knothead up, eyes on
    a butterfly.
This must be perfect progress where
    movement appears
to be a vanishing, a mending
    of the visible

by the invisible—just as we
    stitch the earth,
it seems to me, each time
    we die, going
back under, coming back up. . . .
    It is the simplest

stitch, this going where we must,
    leaving a not
unpretty pattern by default. But going
    out of hunger
for small things—flies, words—going
    because one's body

goes. And in this disconcerting creature
    a tiny hunger,
one that won't even press
    the dandelions down,
retrieves the necessary blue-
    black dragonfly

that has just landed on a pod . . .
    All this to say
I'm not afraid of them
    today, or anymore
I think. We are not, were not, ever
    wrong. Desire

is the honest work of the body,
    its engine, its wind.
It too must have its sails—wings
    in this tiny mouth, valves
in the human heart, meanings like sailboats
    setting out

over the mind. Passion is work
    that retrieves us,
lost stitches. It makes a pattern of us,
    it fastens us
to sturdier stuff
    no doubt.

SALMON

I watched them once, at dusk, on television, run,
in our motel room half-way through
Nebraska, quick, glittering, past beauty, past
the importance of beauty,
archaic,
not even hungry, not even endangered, driving deeper and deeper
into less. They leapt up falls, ladders,
and rock, tearing and leaping, a gold river
and a blue river traveling
in opposite directions.
They would not stop, resolution of will
and helplessness, as the eye
is helpless
when the image forms itself, upside-down, backward,
driving up into
the mind, and the world
unfastens itself
from the deep ocean of the given. . . . Justice, aspen
leaves, mother attempting
suicide, the white night-flying moth
the ants dismantled bit by bit and carried in
right through the crack
in my wall. . . . How helpless
the still pool is,
upstream,
awaiting the gold blade
of their hurry. Once, indoors, a child,
I watched, at noon, through slatted wooden blinds,
a man and woman, naked, eyes closed,
climb onto each other,
on the terrace floor,
and ride—two gold currents
wrapping round and round each other, fastening,
unfastening. I hardly knew

what I saw. Whatever shadow there was in that world
it was the one each cast
onto the other,
the thin black seam
they seemed to be trying to work away
between them. I held my breath.
As far as I could tell, the work they did
with sweat and light
was good. I'd say
they traveled far in opposite
directions. What is the light
at the end of the day, deep, reddish-gold, bathing the walls,
the corridors, light that is no longer light, no longer clarifies,
illuminates, antique, freed from the body of
the air that carries it. What is it
for the space of time
where it is useless, merely
beautiful? When they were done, they made a distance
one from the other
and slept, outstretched,
on the warm tile
of the terrace floor,
smiling, faces pressed against the stone.

HISTORY

Into whose ear the deeds are spoken. The only
listener. So I believed
he would remember everything, the murmuring trees,
the sunshine's zealotry, its deep
unevenness. For history
is the opposite
of the eye
for whom, for instance, six million bodies in portions
of hundreds and
the flowerpots broken by a sudden wind stand as
equivalent. What more
is there
than fact? *I'll give ten thousand dollars to the man
who proves the holocaust really
occurred* said the exhausted solitude
in San Francisco
in 1980. Far in the woods
in a faded photograph
in 1942 the man with his own
genitalia in his mouth and hundreds of
slow holes
a pitchfork has opened
over his face
grows beautiful. The ferns and deepwood
lilies catch
the eye. Three men in ragged uniforms
with guns keep laughing
nervously. They share the day
with him. A bluebird
sings. The feathers of the shade touch every inch
of skin—the hand holding down the delicate gun,
the hands holding down the delicate
hips. And the sky
is visible between the men, between

the trees, a blue spirit
enveloping
anything. Late in the story, in northern Italy,
a man cuts down some trees for winter
fuel. We read this in the evening
news. Watching the fire burn late
one night, watching it change and change, a hand
   grenade,
lodged in the pulp the young tree
grew around, explodes, blinding the man, killing
his wife. Now who
will tell the children
fairytales? The ones where simple
crumbs over the forest
floor endure
to help us home?

Two Paintings by Gustav Klimt

Although what glitters
    on the trees,
row after perfect row,
    is merely
the injustice
    of the world,

the chips on the bark of each
    beech tree
catching the light, the sum
    of these delays
is the beautiful, the human
    beautiful,

body of flaws.
    The dead
would give anything
    I'm sure,
to step again onto
    the leafrot,

into the avenue of mottled shadows,
    the speckled
broken skins. The dead
    in their sheer
open parenthesis, what they
    wouldn't give

for something to lean on
    that won't
give way. I think I
    would weep
for the moral nature

of this world,

for right and wrong like pools
        of shadow
and light you can step in
        and out of
crossing this yellow beech forest,
        this *buchen-wald*,

one autumn afternoon, late
        in the twentieth
century, in hollow light,
        in gaseous light. . . .
To receive the light
        and return it

and stand in rows, anonymous,
        is a sweet secret
even the air wishes
        it could unlock.
See how it pokes at them
        in little hooks,

the blue air, the yellow trees.
        Why be afraid?
They say when Klimt
        died suddenly
a painting, still
        incomplete,

was found in his studio,
        a woman's body
open at its point of
        entry,
rendered in graphic,
        pornographic,

detail—something like
    a scream
between her legs. Slowly,
    feathery,
he had begun to paint
    a delicate

garment (his trademark)
    over this mouth
of her body. The mouth
    of her face
is genteel, bored, feigning a need
    for sleep. The fabric

defines the surface,
    the story,
so we are drawn to it,
    its blues
and yellows glittering
    like a stand

of beech trees late
    one afternoon
in Germany, in fall.
    It is called
Buchenwald, it is
    1890. In

the finished painting
    the argument
has something to do
    with pleasure.

AT LUCA SIGNORELLI'S
RESURRECTION OF THE BODY

See how they hurry
    to enter
their bodies,
    these spirits.
Is it better, flesh,
    that they

should hurry so?
    From above
the green-winged angels
    blare down
trumpets and light. But
    they don't care,

they hurry to congregate,
    they hurry
into speech, until
    it's a marketplace,
it is humanity. But still
    we wonder

in the chancel
    of the dark cathedral,
is it better, back?
    The artist
has tried to make it so: each tendon
    they press

to re-enter
    is perfect. But is it
perfection
    they're after,
pulling themselves up
    through the soil

into the weightedness, the color,
    into the eye
of the painter? Outside
    it is 1500,
all round the cathedral
    streets hurry to open

through the wild
    silver grasses. . . .
The men and women
    on the cathedral wall
do not know how,
    having come this far,

to stop their
    hurrying. They amble off
in groups, in
    couples. Soon
some are clothed, there is
    distance, there is

perspective. Standing below them
    in the church
in Orvieto, how can we
    tell them
to be stern and brazen
    and slow,

that there is no
    entrance,
only entering. They keep on
    arriving,
wanting names,
    wanting

happiness. In his studio
	Luca Signorelli
in the name of God
	and Science
and the believable
	broke into the body

studying arrival.
	But the wall
of the flesh
	opens endlessly,
its vanishing point so deep
	and receding

we have yet to find it,
	to have it
stop us. So he cut
	deeper,
graduating slowly
	from the symbolic

to the beautiful. How far
	is true?
When his one son
	died violently,
he had the body brought to him
	and laid it

on the drawing-table,
	and stood
at a certain distance
	awaiting the best
possible light, the best depth
	of day,

then with beauty and care
	and technique

and judgment, cut into
    shadow, cut
into bone and sinew and every
    pocket

in which the cold light
    pooled.
It took him days,
    that deep
caress, cutting,
    unfastening,

until his mind
    could climb into
the open flesh and
    mend itself.

from

THE END
OF BEAUTY

SELF-PORTRAIT AS THE GESTURE BETWEEN THEM [ADAM AND EVE]

1

The gesture like a fruit torn from a limb, torn swiftly.

2

The whole bough bending then springing back as if from sudden sight.

3

The rip in the fabric where the action begins, the opening of the narrow
passage.

4

The passage along the arc of denouement once the plot has begun, like a limb,
the buds in it cinched and numbered,
outside the true story really, outside of improvisation,
moving along day by day into the sweet appointment.

5

But what else could they have done, these two, sick of beginning,
revolving in place like a thing seen,
dumb, blind, rooted in the eye that's watching,
ridden and ridden by that slowest of glances the passage of time
staring and staring until the entrails show.

6

Every now and then a quick rain for no reason,

7

a wind moving round all sides, a wind shaking the points of view out
like the last bits of rain. . . .

So it was to have freedom she did it but like a secret thought.
A thought of him the light couldn't touch.
The light beating against it, the light flaying her thought of him,
trying to break it.
Like a fruit that grows but only in the invisible.
The whole world of the given beating against this garden
where he walks slowly in the hands of freedom
noiselessly beating his steps against the soil.

9

But a secret grows, a secret wants to be given away.
For a long time it swells and stains its bearer with beauty.
It is what we see swelling forth making the shape we know a thing by.
The thing inside, the critique of the given.

10

So that she turned the thought of him in her narrow mind,
turned him slowly in the shallows, like a thin bird she'd found,
turned him in this place which was her own, as if to plant him but never
letting go,
keeping the thought of him keen and simple in a kind of winter,
keeping him in this shadowlessness in which he needn't breathe,
him turning to touch her as a thing turns towards its thief,
owned but not seizable, resembling, resembling. . . .

11

Meanwhile the heights of things were true. Meanwhile the distance of
the fields was true. Meanwhile the fretting of the light against the backs
of them
as they walked through the fields naming things, true,
the touch of the light along the backs of their bodies . . .

1 2

as the apple builds inside the limb, as rain builds
in the atmosphere, as the lateness accumulates until it finally
is,
as the meaning of the story builds,

1 3

scribbling at the edges of her body until it must be told, be

1 4

taken from her, this freedom,

1 5

so that she had to turn and touch him to give it away

1 6

to have him pick it from her as the answer takes the question

1 7

that he should read in her the rigid inscription

1 8

in a scintillant fold the fabric of the daylight bending

1 9

where the form is complete where the thing must be torn off

2 0

momentarily angelic, the instant writhing into a shape,

the two wedded, the readiness and the instant,

the extra bit that shifts the scales the other way now in his hand,
the gift that changes the balance,

the balance that cannot be broken owned by the air until he touches,

the balance like an apple held up into the sunlight

then taken down, the air changing by its passage, the feeling of being capable,

of being not quite right for the place, not quite the thing that's needed,

the feeling of being a digression not the link in the argument,
a new direction, an offshoot, the limb going on elsewhere,

and liking that error, a feeling of being capable *because* an error,

of being wrong perhaps altogether wrong a piece from another set

stripped of position stripped of true function

31

and loving that error, loving that filial form, that break from perfection

32

where the complex mechanism fails, where the stranger appears in the clearing,

33

out of nowhere and uncalled for, out of nowhere to share the day.

ON DIFFICULTY

It's that they want to know *whose* they are,
seen from above in the half burnt-out half blossomed-out
woods, late April, unsure as to whether to
turn back.
The woods are not their home.
The blossoming is not their home. Whatever's back there
is not. Something floats in the air all round them
as if *it* were the place
where the day drowns,
and the place at the edge of cries, for instance, that fissure, gleams.
Now he's holding his hand out.
Is there a hollow she's the shape of?
And in their temples a thrumming like
what-have-I-done?—but not yet a question, really, not
yet what slips free of the voice to float like a brackish foam
on emptiness—
Oh you will come to it, you two down there
where the vines begin, you will come to it,
the thing towards which you reason, the place where the flotsam
of the meanings is put down
and the shore
holds. They're thinking *we must have slept a while,*
what is it has changed? They're thinking
how low the bushes are, after all, how finite
the options one finds in the
waiting (after all). More like the branchings of whiteness
always stopping short into this shade or that,
breaking inertia then stopping,
breaking the current at last into shape but then
stopping—
If you asked them, where they first find the edges of each other's bodies, *where*
happiness resides they'd look up through the gap
in the greenery you're looking down through.
What they want to know—the icons silent in the shut church (to the left),

the distance silent in the view (to the right)—
is how to give themselves *away*,
which is why they look up now,
which is why they'll touch each other now (for your
looking), which is why they want to know what this
reminds you of
looking up, reaching each other for you to see, for you to see by, the long
sleep
beginning, the long sleep of resemblance,
touching each other further for you that Eternity begin, there, between you,
letting the short jabs of grass hold them up for you to count by,
to color the scene into the believable by,
letting the thousands of individual blossoms add up
and almost (touching her further) block your view of them—
When you look away
who will they be dear god and what?

ORPHEUS AND EURYDICE

Up ahead, I know, he felt it stirring in himself already, the glance,
the darting thing in the pile of rocks,

already in him, there, shiny in the rubble, hissing Did you want to remain
completely unharmed?—

the point-of-view darting in him, shiny head in the ash-heap,

hissing Once upon a time, and then Turn now darling give me that look,

that perfect shot, give me that place where I'm erased. . . .

The thing, he must have wondered, could it be put to rest, there, in the
                                                                glance,
could it lie back down into the dustiness, giving its outline up?

When we turn to them—limbs, fields, expanses of dust called meadow and
                                                                avenue—
will they be freed then to slip back in?

Because you see he could not be married to it anymore, this field with
                                                        minutes in it
called woman, its presence in him the thing called

future—could not be married to it anymore, expanse tugging his mind out
                                                                into it,
tugging the wanting-to-finish out.

What he dreamed of was this road (as he walked on it), this dustiness,
but without their steps on it, their prints, without
song—

What she dreamed, as she watched him turning with the bend in the road
                                                                (can you

understand this?)—what she dreamed

was of disappearing into the seen

not of disappearing, lord, into the real—

And yes she could feel it in him already, up ahead, that wanting-to-turn-and-
cast-the-outline-over-her

by his glance,

sealing the edges down,

saying I know you from somewhere darling, don't I,
saying You're the kind of woman who etcetera—

(Now the cypress are swaying) (Now the lake in the distance)
(Now the view-from-above, the aerial attack of *do you
remember?*)—

now the glance reaching her shoreline wanting only to be recalled,
now the glance reaching her shoreline wanting only to be taken in,

(somewhere the castle above the river)

(somewhere you holding this piece of paper)

(what will you do next?) (—feel it beginning?)

now she's raising her eyes, as if pulled from above,

now she's looking back into it, into the poison the beginning,

giving herself to it, looking back into the eyes,

feeling the dry soft grass beneath her feet for the first time now the mind looking into that which sets the _____ in motion and seeing in there

a doorway open nothing on either side
(a slight wind now around them, three notes from up the hill)

through which morning creeps and the first true notes—

For they were deep in the earth and what is possible swiftly took hold.

TO THE READER

I swear to you she wanted back into the shut, the slow,

a ground onto which to say This is my actual life, Good Morning,
onto which to say That girl on her knees who is me
is still digging that square yard of land up
to catalogue and press onto the page *all she could find in it*
and name, somewhere late April, where they believe in ideas,
Thursday, a little of what persists and all the rest.

Before that, dreams. The dream of being warm
and staying warm. The dream of the upper hand like a love song,
the dream of the right weapon and then the perfect escape.

Then the dream of the song of having *business* here.

Then the dream of you two sitting on the couch, of the mood
of armies (hand of God), of the city burning in the distance.

The dream of before and after (are we getting closer?) the dream
of *finally after days.* . . .

(Miss _____ lets out a shattering scream.)

I swear to you this begins with that girl on a day after sudden rain
and then out of nowhere sun (as if to expose *what* of the hills—
the white glare of x, the scathing splendor of y,
the wailing interminable _____?) that girl having run
down from the house and up over the fence not like an animal
but like a thinking, link by link, and over

into the allotted earth—for Science Fair—into the everything of
one square yard of earth. Here it begins
to slip. She took the spade and drew the lines. Right through
the weedbeds, lichen, moss, keeping the halves of things that landed *in*

by chance, new leaves, riffraff the wind blew in—

Here is the smell of earth being cut, the smell of the four lines.
Here is the brownsweet of the abstract where her four small furrows
say the one word over.
She will take the ruler and push it down till it's all the way in.
She will slide its razor-edge along through colonies, tunnels,
through powdered rock and powdered leaf,

and everything on its way to the one right destination
like a cloak coming off, shoulders rising,
(after one has abandoned the idea of x;
after one has accorded to the reader the y)—
her hole in the loam like a saying in the midst of the field of patience,
fattening the air above it with detail,
an embellishment on the April air,
the rendezvous of hands and earth—

Say we leave her there, squatting down, haunches up,
pulling the weeds up with tweezers,
pulling the thriving apart into the true,
each seedpod each worm on the way down retrieved into a
plastic bag (shall I compare thee), Say we

leave her there, where else is there to go? A word,
a mouth over water? Is there somewhere
neither there nor here?
Where do we continue living now, in what terrain?
Mud, ash, _____, _____ . We want it to stick to us,
hands not full but not clean. What is wide-meshed enough
yet lets nothing through, the bunch of ribbon,
her hair tied up that the wind be seen?

If, for instance, *this* was the place instead,

where the gods fought the giants and monsters
(us the ideal countryside, flesh, interpretation),

if, for instance, this were not a chosen place but a place
blundered into, a place which is a meadow with a hole in it,

and some crawl through such a hole to the other place

and some use it to count with and buy with

and some hide in it and see Him go by

and to some it is the hole on the back of the man running

through which what's coming towards him is coming into him, growing larger,

a hole in his chest through which the trees in the distance are seen
growing larger shoving out sky shoving out storyline

until it's close it's all you can see this moment this hole in his back

in which now a girl with a weed and a notebook appears.

VERTIGO

Then they came to the very edge of the cliff and looked down.
Below, a real world flowed in its parts, green, green.
The two elements touched—rock, air.
She thought of where the mind opened out
into the sheer drop of its intelligence,
the updrafting pastures of the vertical in which a bird now rose,
blue body the blue wind was knifing upward
faster than it could naturally rise,
up into the downdraft until it was frozen until she could see them
                                                                    at last
the stages of flight, broken down, broken free,
each wingflap folding, each splay of the feather-sets flattening
for entry. . . . *Parts* she thought, *free* parts, watching the laws
at work, *through which desire must course*
seeking an ending, seeking a shape. Until the laws of flight and fall
                                                        increased.
Until they made, all of an instant, a bird, a blue
enchantment of properties no longer
knowable. What is it to understand, she let fly,
leaning outward from the edge now that the others had gone down.
How close can the two worlds get, the movement from one to the other
being death? She tried to remember from the other life
the passage of the rising notes off the violin
into the air, thin air, chopping their way in,
wanting to live forever—marrying, marrying—yet still free of the
                                            orchestral swelling
which would at any moment pick them up, in-
corporate. How is it one soul wants to be owned
by a single other
in its entirety?—
What is it sucks one down, offering itself, only itself, for
ever? She saw the cattle below
moving in a shape which was exactly their hunger.
She saw—could they be men?—the plot. She leaned. How does one enter

a story? Where the cliff and air pressed the end of each other,
everything else in the world—woods, fields, stream, start of another

                                                darker

woods—appeared as kinds of
falling. She listened for the wind again. What was it in there

                                        she could hear

that has nothing to do with *telling the truth*?
What was it that was *not her listening*?
She leaned out. What is it pulls at one, she wondered,
what? That it has no shape but point of view?
That it cannot move to hold us?
Oh it has vibrancy, she thought, this emptiness, this intake just

                                    prior to

the start of a story, the mind trying to fasten
and fasten, the mind feeling it like a sickness this wanting
to snag, catch hold, begin, the mind crawling out to the edge of the cliff
and feeling the body as if for the first time—how it cannot
follow, cannot love.

WHAT THE END IS FOR

[GRAND FORKS, NORTH DAKOTA]

A boy just like you took me out to see them,
    the five hundred B-52's on alert on the runway,
fully loaded fully manned pointed in all the directions,
    running every minute
of every day.
    They sound like a sickness of the inner ear,

where the heard foams up into the noise of listening,
    where the listening arrives without being extinguished.
The huge hum soaks up into the dusk.
    The minutes spring open. Six is too many.
From where we watch,
    from where even watching is an anachronism,

from the 23rd of March from an open meadow,
    the concertina wire in its double helix
designed to tighten round a body if it turns
    is the last path the sun can find to take out,
each barb flaring gold like a braille being read,
    then off with its knowledge and the sun
is gone. . . .

That's when the lights on all the extremities, like an outline, like a dress,
    become loud in the story,
and a dark I have not seen before
    sinks in to hold them one
by one.
    Strange plot made to hold so many inexhaustible
screams.
    Have you ever heard in a crowd mutterings of
blame

that will not modulate that will not rise?
     He tells me, your stand-in, they *stair-step* up.
He touches me to have me look more deeply
     in
to where for just a moment longer
     color still lives:
the belly white so that it looks like sky, the top
     some kind of brown, some soil—How does it look

from up there now
     this meadow we lie on our bellies in, this field Iconography
tells me stands for sadness
     because the wind can move through it uninterrupted?
What is it the wind
     would have wanted to find and didn't

leafing down through this endless admiration unbroken
     because we're too low for it
to find us?
     Are you still there for me now in that dark
we stood in for hours
     letting it sweep as far as it could down over us
unwilling to move, irreconcilable? What *he*
     wants to tell me,

his whisper more like a scream
     over this eternity of engines never not running,
is everything: how the crews assigned to each plane
     for a week at a time, the seven boys, must live
inseparable,
     how they stay together for life,
how the wings are given a life of
     seven feet of play,

how they drop practice bombs called shapes over Nevada,
     how the measures for counterattack in air
have changed and we

now forego firepower for jamming, for the throwing
of false signals. The meadow, the meadow hums, love, with the planes,
    as if every last blade of grass were wholly possessed

by this practice, wholly prepared. The last time I saw you,
    we stood facing each other as dusk came on.
I leaned against the refrigerator, you leaned against the door.
    The picture window behind you was slowly extinguished,
the tree went out, the two birdfeeders, the metal braces on them.
    The light itself took a long time,

bits in puddles stuck like the useless
    splinters of memory, the chips
of history, hopes, laws handed down. *Here, hold these* he says, these
    grasses these
torn pods, he says, smiling over the noise another noise, *take these*
    he says, my hands wrong for

the purpose, here,
    not-visible-from-the-sky, prepare yourself with these, boy and
bouquet of
    thistleweed and wort and william and
timothy. We stood there. Your face went out a long time
    before the rest of it. Can't see you anymore I said. *Nor I,*
you, whatever you still were
    replied.
When I asked you to hold me you refused.
    When I asked you to cross the six feet of room to hold me

you refused. Until I
    couldn't rise out of the patience either any longer
to make us
    take possession.
Until we were what we must have wanted to be:
    shapes the shapelessness was taking back.
Why should I lean out?
    Why should I move?

When the Maenads tear Orpheus limb from limb,
    they throw his head

out into the river.
    Unbodied it sings
all the way downstream, all the way to the single ocean,
    head floating in current downriver singing,
until the sound of the cataracts grows,
    until the sound of the open ocean grows and the voice.

SELF-PORTRAIT
AS APOLLO AND DAPHNE

1

The truth is this had been going on for a long time during which
    they both wanted it to last.

You can still hear them in that phase, the north and
south laid up against each other, constantly erasing
each minute with each minute.

You can still hear them, there, just prior to daybreak,
the shrill cheeps and screeches of the awakening thousands,
hysterical, for miles, in all the directions,

and there the whoo whoo of the nightfeeders, insolvent baseline,
shorn, almost the sound of thin air. . . .

Or there where the sun picks up on the bits of broken glass
throughout the miles of grass for just a fraction of an instant
(thousands of bits) at just one angle, quick, the evidence,
    the landfill,
then gone again, everything green, green. . . .

2

How he wanted, though, to possess her, to nail the erasures,

3

like a long heat on her all day once the daysounds set in, like
a long analysis.

4

The way she kept slipping away was this: can you really
see me, can you really know I'm really who . . .
His touchings a rhyme she kept interrupting (no one
believes in that version anymore she whispered, no one
can hear it anymore, *tomorrow, tomorrow,*
like the different names of those girls
all one girl). . . . But how long could it
last?

He kept after her like sunlight (it's not what you think, she said)
frame after frame of it (it's not what you think you think)
like the prayer that numbers are praying (are they ascending are they
descending?)

He kept after her in the guise of the present,
minute after minute (are they ascending are they?)
until they seemed to quicken and narrow (like footprints

piling up, like footprints all blurred at the end of, at the scene of . . .)

until *now is forever* he whispered can't you get it to open,

present tense without end, slaughtered motion, kingdom of
heaven?—

the shards caught here and there—*what did you do
before?* or *will you forgive me?* or *say
that you'll love me for
ever and ever*

(is it a squeal of brakes is it a birthcry?)

(let x equal forever he whispered let y let y . . .)

7

as opposed to that other motion which reads Cast it upon the ground
and it shall become a serpent (and Moses fled before it),
which reads Put forth thy hand and take it by the tail
and it was a rod in his hand again—

8

That's when she stopped, she turned her face to the wind, shut her eyes—

9

She stopped she turned,
she would not be the end towards which he was ceaselessly tending,
she would not give shape to his hurry by being
        its destination,
it was wrong this progress, it was a quick iridescence
on the back of some other thing, unimaginable, a flash on the wing of . . .

1 0

The sun would rise and the mind would rise
and the will would rise and the eyes—The eyes—:
the whole of the story like a transcript of sight,
of the distance between them, the small gap he would close.

1 1

She would stop, there would be no chase scene, she would
        be who,
what?

1 2

The counting went on all round like a thousand birds
each making its own wind—who would ever add them up?—

and what would the sum become, of these minutes, each flapping
its wings, each after a perch,

each one with its call going unanswered,

each one signaling separately into the end of the daybreak,

the great screech of the instants, the pileup,
the one math of hope, the prayer nowhere is praying,

frame after frame, collision of tomorrows—

No she would go under, she would leave him the freedom

his autograph all over it, slipping, trying to notch it,

13

there in the day with him now, his day, but altered,

14

part of the view not one of the actors, she thought,
not one of the instances, not one of the examples,

15

but the air the birds call in,
the air their calls going unanswered marry in,
the calls the different species make, cross-currents, frettings,
and the one air holding the screeching separateness—
each wanting to change, to be heard, to have been changed—
and the air all round them neither full nor empty,
but holding them, holding them, untouched, untransformed.

THE LOVERS

They have been staring at each other for a long time now.
Around them the objects (circa 1980).
Then corridors, windows, a meadow, the _____ .
They have been staring at the end of each other for a long
time now.
She tries to remember but it is hopeless.
She tries the other one—Hope—casting outward
        a bit,
oh but it costs too much.
Either they're coming for us now or they're not says Love.
Around them objects, minutes, *No* said quickly in passing.
Here it is, *here,* the end of beauty, the present.
What the vista fed into. What it wants to grow out of, creeping,
        succulent. . . .
No No says the voice pinpointing the heart of these
        narrows.
Draw draw the curtain now.
You there in your seat, you there.
Here is the glance, between them, quick, the burning.
Here is the glance afloat—on the back of what, dear nothingness?
Here it is, here—
They've decided they'll feed everything into it and then they'll see.
They've decided they want the rest tight round them now like
        this.
They want to be owned, it is all that can own them.
The look, the look finally free of the anything looked-for,
the hurry finally come unstuck of the hurrying,
something fiery all around like dust or a jury.
You there. They are done talking.
They are done waiting.
Either they are or they're not, she thinks, hold still.
Something fiery all round—let it
        decide.
It will need us to shape it (won't it?)   hold still.

74

And the cries increasingly   hold still.
Like a _____ this look between us   hold still.
If, inside, a small terrified happiness begins,
like an idea of color,
like an idea of color sinking to stain an instance, a *thing,*
like an arm holding a lit candle in a door that is parting,
if, oh if—banish it.
Listen, this is the thing that can trap it now—the glance—
the howling and biting gap—
and our two faces raised
that nothing begin (don't look away),
that there be no elsewhere,
that there be no elsewhere to seed out into,
just this here between us, this look (can you see me?), this
        look afloat on want,
this long thin angel whose body is a stalk, rootfree,
        blossomfree,
whose body we are making, whose body is a _____
(only quicker, much quicker, a conflagration)
an angel, the last one, the only one that can still live
        here
(while out in the corridor they are taking down names)
(while out in the corridor the shoes purr for the blacking)
the last one, the very last,
alive, yes—yes—but wingless this *between,* wingless—

NOLI ME TANGERE

1

You see the angels have come to sit on the delay
    for a while,
they have come to harrow the fixities, the sharp edges
    of this open
sepulcher,
    they have brought their swiftnesses like musics

down
    to fit them on the listening.
Their robes, their white openmindedness gliding into the corners,
    slipping this way then that
over the degrees, over the marble

flutings.
    The small angelic scripts pressing up through the veils.
The made shape pressing
    up through the windy cloth.
I've watched all afternoon how the large
    red birds here

cross and recross neither for play nor hunger
    the gaps that constitute our chainlink fence,
pressing themselves narrowly against the metal,
    feeding their bodies and wings
tightly in.
    Out of what ceases into what is ceasing.
Out of the light which holds steel and its alloys,

into the words for it like some robe or glory,
    and all of this rising up into the deep unbearable thinness,
the great babyblue exhalation of the one God
    as if in satisfaction at some right ending
come,

76

then down onto the dustiness that still somehow holds
    its form as downslope and new green meadow
through which at any moment
    something swifter
might cut.
    It is about to be
Spring.
    The secret cannot be

kept.
    It wants to cross over, it wants
to be a lie.

2

Is that it then? Is that the law of freedom?
    That she must see him yet must not touch?
Below them the soldiers sleep their pure deep sleep.
    Is he light
who has turned forbidding and thrust his hand up
    in fury,

is he flesh
    so desperate to escape, to carry his purpose away?
She wants to put her hands in,
    she wants to touch him.
He wants her to believe,
    who has just trusted what her eyes have given her,

he wants her to look away.
    I've listened where the words and the minutes would touch,
I've tried to hear in that slippage what
    beauty is—
her soil, his sweet tune like footsteps
    over the path of

least resistance. I can see
  the body composed
of the distance between them.
  I know it is ours: he must change, she must
remember.
  But you see it is not clear to me why she

must be driven back,
  why it is the whole darkness that belongs to her
and its days,
  why it is these hillsides she must become,
supporting even now the whole weight of the weightless,
  letting the plotlines wander all over her,

crumbling into every digressive beauty,
  her longings all stitchwork towards his immaculate rent,
all alphabet on the wind as she rises from prayer. . . .

3

It is the horror, Destination,
  pulling the whole long song
down, like a bad toss
  let go
in order to start again right,
  and it is wrong

to let its one inaudible note govern our going
  isn't it, siren over this open meadow
singing always your one song of shape of
  home. I have seen how the smoke here
inhabits a space
  in the body of air it must therefore displace,

and the tree-shaped gap the tree inhabits,
  and the tree-shaped gap the tree

invents. Siren,
    reader,
it is here, only here,
    in this gap

between us,
    that the body of who we are
to have been
    emerges: imagine:
she lets him go,
    she lets him through the day faster than the day,

among the brisk wings
    upsetting the flowerpots,
among the birds arranging and rearranging the shape of
    the delay,
she lets him
    slip free,

letting him posit the sweet appointment,
    letting out that gold thread that crazy melody
of stations,
    reds, birds, dayfall, screen-door,
desire,

until you have to go with him, don't you,

until you have to leave her be
    if all you have to touch her with
is form.

SELF-PORTRAIT AS HURRY AND DELAY [PENELOPE AT HER LOOM]

1

So that every night above them in her chambers she unweaves it.
Every night by torchlight under the flitting shadows the postponement,
working her fingers into the secret place, the place of what is coming
    undone,

2

to make them want her more richly, there, where the pattern softens now,
    loosening,

3

to see what was healed under there by the story when it lifts,
by color and progress and motive when they lift,

4

the bandage the history gone into thin air,

5

to have them for an instant in her hands both at once,
the story and its undoing, the days the kings and the soil they're groundcover
    for

6

all winter,

7

against choice against offspring against the minutes like turrets
building the walls, the here and the there, in which he wanders searching,

till it lifts and the mouth of something fangs open there,
and the done and the undone rush into each other's arms.
A *mouth* or a gap in the fleshy air, a place in both worlds.
A woman's body, a spot where a story now gone has ridden.
The yarn springing free.
The opening trembling, the nothing, the nothing with use in it trembling—

9

Oh but is it wide enough to live on, immaculate present tense, lull
    between wars,

1 0

the threads running forwards yet backwards over her stilled fingers,

1 1

the limbs of the evergreens against the windowpane, the thousand hands,
beating then touching then suddenly still for no reason?

1 2

Reader, minutes:

1 3

now her fingers dart like his hurry darts over this openness he can't
    find the edge of,
like the light over the water seeking the place on the water
where out of air and point-of-view and roiling wavetips a shapeliness,
    a possession of happiness
forms,

a body of choices among the waves, a strictness among them, an edge
    to the light,

something that is not something else,

14

until she knows he's here who wants to be trapped in here,
her hands tacking his quickness down as if soothing it to sleep,
the threads carrying the quickness in on their backs,
burying it back into there, into the pattern, the noble design,
like a stain they carry past a sleeping giant,
the possible like kindling riding in on their backs,
the flames enlarging and gathering on the walls,
wanting to be narrowed, rescued, into a story again, a transparence we
can't see through, a lover

15

approaching ever approaching the unmade beneath him,
knotting and clasping it within his motions,
wrapping himself plot plot and denouement over the roiling openness. . . .

16

Yet what would she have if he were to arrive?
Sitting enthroned what would either have?
It is his wanting in the threads she has to keep alive for him,
scissoring and spinning and pulling the long minutes free, it is

17

the shapely and mournful delay she keeps alive for him the breathing

18

as the long body of the beach grows emptier awaiting him

19

gathering the holocaust in close to its heart growing more beautiful

20

under the meaning under the soft hands of its undoing

saying Goodnight goodnight for now going upstairs

under the kissing of the minutes under the wanting to go on living

beginning always beginning the ending as they go to sleep beneath her.

BREAKDANCING

[TERESA: SAINT TERESA OF ÁVILA]

Staying alive the boy on the screen is doing it,
    the secret nobody knows like a rapture through his limbs,
the secret, *the robot-like succession of joint isolations*
    that simulate a body's reaction to
electric shock.
    This is how it tells itself: pops, ticks, waves and the

float. What
    is poverty for, Mr. Speed, Dr. Cadet, Dr. Rage,
Timex? Don't push me the limbs are whispering, don't push
    'cause I'm close to the edge the footwork is whispering
down onto the sidewalk that won't give in won't go some other
    where while the TV

hums and behind me their breathings, husband, daughter, too slow,
    go in to that other place and come back out
unstained, handfuls at a time, air, air—
    The flag of the greatest democracy on earth
waves in the wind with the sound turned off. The current

rubs through the stars and stripes
    like a muttering passing through a crowd and coming out an
anthem,
    string of words on its search
and destroy
    needing bodies, bodies. . . .
I'm listening to where she must not choke. I'm listening
    to where he must not be betrayed. I'm trying

to hear pity, the idiom. I'm trying to lean into those
    marshes and hear
what comes through clean,

what comes through changed,
having needed us.

    Oh but you must not fail to eat and sleep Teresa murmurs to
her flock,

staying alive is the most costly gift you have to offer Him—all the while
                                   watching,

    (whispering *Lord, what will you have me*
do?) for his corporeal
    appearance
in the light of sixteenth century, in the story that flutters
    blowzy over the body of the land
we must now somehow ram
    the radioactive waste

into. He
    showed himself to her in pieces.
First the fingertips, there in mid-air,
    clotting, floating, held up by the invisible, neither rising
nor falling nor approaching nor lingering, then hands, then a

few days later feet, torso, then arms, each part alone, each part
    free of its argument, then days, then eyes,
then face entire, then days again, then *His*
    most sacred humanity in its risen form
was represented to me

completely. "Don't try
    to hold me in yourself (the air, hissing) but try to hold yourself
in me," Nov 18, 1570. I'm listening to where she must not choke,
    I'm listening to where he must not, must not. . . . Air,
holding a girl in a man's arms now,
    making them look like wind,
what if they can't be returned to you
    the *things* now reaching me—the three

exhalings, hum, blue light, the minutes, the massacres, the strict halflife of
	radioactive isotopes, the shallow
graves, the seventeen rememberable personal
	lies? What if they go only this far, grounding
in me, staying
	alive?
Here is the secret: the end is an animal.
	Here is the secret: the end is an animal growing by

accretion, image by image, vote by
	vote. *No more pain* hums the air,
as the form of things shall have fallen
		from thee, no more pain, just the here and the now, the jackpot, the
watching, minutes exploding like thousands of silver dollars all over your
		face your hands but tenderly, almost tenderly, turning mid-air, gleaming,
so slow, as if it could last,
	frame after frame of nowhere

turning into the living past.

THE VEIL

In the Tabernacle the veil hangs which is (choose one):
the dress dividing us from _____ ; the sky; the real,
through which the x ascends (His feet still showing through on
                                    this side)
into the realm of uncreated things,
up, swift as proof,
leaving behind this *red* over our row of poplars now,
then just the poplars
a while longer,
then what we know as *gone*—the sky brightest for an instant
where a single motorcycle sputters
backfiring once.
Why this sudden silence?
What is the street, the time of day?
What is that young kid cruising towards against such minutes?
And the first person is where, please, in this place, pushing
      and watching?
Will the windows remain open much longer?
Will the mention of death occur even if only
once? And the cramped orchard of seven trees, soot-burnt,
above the traintracks, will it come to
stand for loss or only how knowledge lingers
against the linear? A train can be heard
(there is distance), and a voice calling an *Andrew* in
because the dampness, yes, is setting in and because no matter what
I'd do, unfinishing, the damp—as soon as sunlight's
gone—has rights in the matter even the author does not have
and the mother, calling and calling, knows this
who has been reading the same page over and over
                        all afternoon
in her kitchen until it's darker than she thought
and still she won't get up.
Oh but you've seen her before, haven't you,
sitting at the table letting dusk come on,

unable to rise, flick the switch, let the new version
in.
It's that she wants to be free.
It's that she wants to be something the day must cross
not someone left to cross the day
along with the rest of the things.
Andrew is elsewhere (not even here). Andrew
is letting himself slip again and again
over a slick downleaning patch of moss the hill above the traintracks
owns. When he puts his hands in it he knows what
a *version* is, although he'd say to you, approaching in the evening,
that it *feels good* as the beginning of a story
feels good
just where it starts to freeze against the banks of
what it's not—
You see, there *is* a veil, or no, there is no veil but
there is
a rip in the veil,
which is the storyline,
what the lips just inconceivably apart can make
that cannot then, ever again, be uncreated—
(and then she wept) (and then a second backfire now at x remove)—
On the one side the tearing (the story)
on the other the torn (what it lets shine
through) and in between the veil being rent *(for all
eternity)* by this place made of words,
the gap her calling
would extinguish,
the mother of this story
—Because you see she is still calling,
bless her, she has an appointment for you to keep
and an indoors in which to keep it,
a stillness of place and circumstance which begins
when the lights go on and questions for which there are no answers
are asked out of kindness
and *love*—which is the stillest motion gets,
which is what description is as it reaches a listener,

88

love, in which the room is airy and light and open against change,
in which the room is exactly what you meant to say
(while across the street of course. . . .) (I'm writing this now lying

down, I'm

writing this now
into the mirror—can I take it from you, what would it take?)
love which is the mother calling you in and you going
so that this can have really happened and you
not know of the afternoon, for example, darkening where she read
the same page over and over for no reason,
the nothing-but-life sticky all over the walls,
the nothing-on-the-page swallowing the walls and so on
next to the photograph of her next to the fountain once—
You running up the stairs now into her
Good Evening Darling like an idea come back to life
where the ink dries, the body disappears, one more chair
is added,
you rushing in to be a point of view, wanting to live more deeply from

now on,

to live somewhere *else*,
though not yet (dear x) not yet—

IMPERIALISM

Nothing but a shadow, lord, and hazy at that, at my feet,
    that not even the dust and the gravel can hold.
And when a birdcall happens
    can it (anywhere) intersect with the shadow or the gravel or the
voice stuttering somewhere above it *foxglove blooms* and then
    wind blows to bend the foxglove all one way?

I can see the wind in the hair of the shadow.
    I can see its sleeve flutter from torn to whole and back
in a flash.
    Now it coats a bank of stonecrop, a butterfly, a hole where a rock
someone lifted is
    missing,

now it returns them to the sun, unchanged.
    What I want to know, dear are-you-there,
is what it *is,* this life a shadow and a dust-road have,
    the shape constantly laying herself down over the sparkling dust
she cannot own—
    What can they touch of one another, and what is it *for*

this marriage, this life of Look, here's a body, now here's
    a body, now here,
here. . . .
    Last night I watched your face in the lamplight fluttering—
We were trying to talk—The kerosene was thinning—

You never had your face but something like cleared light then
    soiled light
(roiling)
    and on it all—imprint that would not take—eyeholes, mouth
hole. There were moths.
    There were foodstains my fingers found in the woodgrain.
Later there were cruelties exchanged

between us.
Once you stood up grabbed your hat put it back down.
    When you sat down again we were not free.

There was a space across which you and your shadow, pacing,
    broke,
and around you pockets of shadow, sucking, shutting.
    By now the talk had changed.
There was a liquid of wall and stove and space-behind-the-stove.
    And x where the mirror had been.
And x where the window had been.
    And x where my hand slid over the tabletop breaking a glass.

There were shadows in the shadows, and in there were cuts.

    It took all that we are
to keep the thing clear—the narrative of
    bentwood chair and hinge and trim where the linoleum
grips. . . .
    We sat in the one world and let her seep on into us, old hag,
all holes—
    What would she be
without us

willing to sit and clarify and try to nail

it shut? We give her that glitzy fluttering, her body, by the one deep-driven
    nail of point-of-view,
don't we? And there was a story I wanted
    to tell you then but couldn't
(just where she came on into us and we pushed back with
    better rephrasings) (dear Cinderella) (Dear Cinderella our shut eyes restore

to ash) there was a story
    about how as a child Mother took me to see
the great river Ganges
    in the Imperial city of Calcutta. Dear secret,

what was it I saw?
>On the one bank (our bank)

bodies crushed, teeming, washing their knives, themselves, their sick,
>and linens, and dishes, and newborn
calves—tens and hundreds of thousands of bodies mostly
>wet and partly naked even now pressing to get to
waterfront

in a hot sun the river thou shalt not step into twice dear god
>utensils and genitalia and incandescent linens—(I was nine)—.
Not far upriver were the pyres, and because she wished for me
>to *know the world*:
we had watched a number of bodies (of burnings) that morning

then watched the pulleys lift
>the fine-meshed grille covered with ash and cartilage
down into the river
>and shake it, and shake it (at the end of its chains).
It was near noon. I watched its pattern which told a story
>in metal and held a tree and heaven and two animals

beside the naked woman's shape
>shudder in the river as if to imprint it
and then submerge (no trace) then rise back up
>and something like a tree and haunches reappear
on the face of the waters.
>Later she had me walk on in.
Strange water. Thick. I can recall it even now. The more
>it slipped off you the more it clung to you
and caked

so that the only sense of cleanliness you got
>was in the decision
to stop
>and let the sun reclaim you, and let it seal the film of silt

down tight.
    Of course we showered in the hotel.
Why does this matter now?
    I know I didn't even touch that place. That it's *exotic*

even now, and here, whatever imagery might
    be of use. What is the usery that's deep enough?
The story goes I cried so much in the hotel that night
    they had to call whatever doctor was on hand
to give me a shot of what?—probably Demerol—
    to stop the screaming. She
tried to hold me to her, I'm sure,

making it worse,
    since her body (in particular) was
no longer relevant. I remember
    looking up out of the water
and seeing that the other bank although quite far away
    was visible
and utterly blank—
    —not one face, rock, tree, hut, road, tent, sign—
just haze and flat—a line drawn simply to finish

the river, to make that motion *seem a river*—
    There must have been trees—no? sacred cows?
I looked up, nine years of age, soaking wet,
    the bodies of all those strangers against me—
(you can't tip forward, you have to sink down)—
    and over there seeing it, whatever it was,

like a held breath over there, like a mouth held agape with
    hesitation? delay? like a listening that has just ceased
over there. . . .
    Of course I know, since, there are reasons
it remain so uninhabited, that bank, I know since it's
    a law—But what I remembered last night to tell you

is a white umbrella a man in the river near me was washing
    and how the dark brown ash-thick riverwater rode
in the delicate tines as he raised it rinsing.
    How he opened and shut it. Opened and shut it.
First near the surface then underwater—

—*first near the surface then underwater*—
    And as for her body ("no longer relevant")
it became nothing to me after that, or something less,
    because I saw what it was, her body, you see—a line
brought round, all the way round, reader, a plot, a
    shape, one of the finished things, one of the

beauties (hear it click shut?) a thing

completely narrowed down to love—all arms, all arms extended in the
    pulsing sticky heat, fan on, overhead on, all
arms no face at all dear god, all arms—

OF FORCED SIGHTES AND
TRUSTY FEREFULNESS

Stopless wind, here are the columbine seeds I have
collected. What we would do with them is
different. Though both your trick and mine flowers blue
and white

with four stem tails and yellow underpetals. Stopless
and unessential, half-hiss, half-
lullaby, if I fell in among your laws,
if I fell down into your mind, your snow, into the miles

of spirit-drafts you drive, frenetic multitudes,
out from the timber to the open ground and back to no
avail, if I fell down, warmblooded, ill, into your endless
evenness,

into this race you start them on and will not let them win . . . ?
If I fell in?
What is your law to my law, unhurried hurrying?
At my remove from you, today, in your supremest

calculation, re-
adjustment, are these three birds scratching for dead
bark beetles, frozen seeds, too late for being here yet only
    here,
in the stenchfree

cold. This is another current, river of rivers, this thrilling
third-act love. Who wouldn't want to stay
behind? They pack the rinds away, the blazing applecores,
the frantic shadow-wings scribbling the fenceposts, window-

panes. Meanwhile you turn, white jury, draft, away,

deep justice done.
I don't presume to cross the distances, the clarity,
but what grows in your only open hands? Or is

digressive love,
row after perfect greenhouse row,
the garden you're out of for good, wind of the theorems,
of proof, square root of light,

chaos of truth,
blinder than the mice that wait you out
        in any crack?
This is the best I can do now for prayer—to you,
for you—these scraps I throw

my lonely acrobats
that fall
of your accord
right to my windowsill: they pack it away, the grains, the

accidents, they pack it deep into the rent
heart of the blue
spruce, skins in with spiky needles. . . . Oh
        hollow
charged with forgetfulness,

through wind, through winter nights, we'll pass,
steering with crumbs, with words,
making of every hour
a thought, remembering

by pain and rhyme and arabesques of foraging
the formula for theft
under your sky that keeps
sliding away

married to hurry
and grim song.

96

from

REGION OF
UNLIKENESS

FISSION

The real electric lights light upon the full-sized
screen
    on which the greater-than-life-size girl appears,
almost nude on the lawn—sprinklers on—
    voice-over her mother calling her name out—loud—
camera angle giving her lowered lids their full
    expanse—a desert—as they rise

out of the shabby annihilation,
    out of the possibility of never-having-been-seen,
and rise,
    till the glance is let loose into the auditorium,
and the man who has just stopped in his tracks
    looks down
for the first

    time. Tick tock. It's the birth of the mercantile
dream (he looks down). It's the birth of
    the dream called
new world (looks down). She lies there. A corridor of light
                            filled with dust
    flows down from the booth to the screen.
Everyone in here wants to be taken off

    somebody's list, wants to be placed on
somebody else's list.
    Tick. It is 1963. The idea of history is being
outmaneuvered.
    So that as the houselights come on—midscene—
not quite killing the picture which keeps flowing beneath,

    a man comes running down the aisle
asking for our attention—
    Ladies and Gentlemen.
I watch the houselights lap against the other light—the tunnel

of image-making dots licking the white sheet awake—
a man, a girl, her desperate mother—daisies growing in the
                                        corner—

        I watch the light from our real place
suck the arm of screen-building light into itself
            until the gesture of the magic forearm frays,
and the story up there grays, pales—them almost lepers now,
                                        saints, such
white on their flesh in
        patches—her thighs like receipts slapped down on a
                                    slim silver tray,

her eyes as she lowers the heart-shaped shades,
        as the glance glides over what used to be the open,
the free,
        as the glance moves, pianissimo, over the glint of day,
over the sprinkler, the mother's voice shrieking like a grappling
        hook,
the grass blades aflame with being-seen, here on the out-

        skirts. . . . You can almost hear the click at the heart of
                                    the silence
where the turnstile shuts and he's *in*—our hero—
        the moment spoked,
our gaze on her fifteen-foot eyes,
        the man hoarse now as he waves his arms,
as he screams to the booth to cut it, cut the sound,
        and the sound is cut,
and her sun-barred shoulders are left to turn

soundless as they accompany
        her neck, her face, the
looking-up.
        Now the theater's skylight is opened and noon slides in.
I watch as it overpowers the electric lights,
        whiting the story out one layer further

100

till it's just a smoldering of whites
        where she sits up, and her stretch of flesh
is just a roiling up of graynesses,
        vague stutterings of
light with motion in them, bits of moving zeros

in the infinite virtuality of light,
        some *likeness* in it but not particulate,
a grave of possible shapes called *likeness*—see it?—something
        scrawling up there that could be skin or daylight or even

the expressway now that he's gotten her to leave with him—
        (it happened rather fast) (do you recall)—

the man up front screaming the President's been shot, waving
        his hat, slamming one hand flat
over the open
        to somehow get
our attention,

in Dallas, behind him the scorcher—whites, grays,
        laying themselves across his face—
him like a beggar in front of us, holding his hat—
        I don't recall what I did,
I don't recall what the right thing to do would be,
        I wanted someone to love. . . .

        There is a way she lay down on that lawn
to begin with,
        in the heart of the sprinklers,
before the mother's call,
        before the man's shadow laid itself down,

there is a way to not yet be wanted,

        there is a way to lie there at twenty-four frames
per second—no faster—

101

not at the speed of plot,
not at the speed of desire—
          the road out—expressway—hotels—motels—
no telling what we'll have to see next,
          no telling what all we'll have to want next,
(right past the stunned rows of houses),
          no telling what on earth we'll have to marry marry marry. . . .

Where the three lights merged:
          where the image licked my small body from the front, the story
                                                            playing
all over my face my
          forwardness,
where the electric lights took up the back and sides,
          the unwavering houselights,
seasonless,

          where the long thin arm of day came in from the top
to touch my head,
          reaching down along my staring face—
where they flared up around my body unable to

merge into each other
          over my likeness,
slamming down one side of me, unquenchable—here static

          there flaming—
sifting grays into other grays—
          mixing the split second into the long haul—
flanking me—undressing something there where my
          body is
though not my body—
          where they play on the field of my willingness,

where they kiss and brood, filtering each other to no avail,
          all over my solo

appearance,
     bits smoldering under the shadows I make—
and aimlessly—what we call *free*—there

the immobilism sets in,
     the being-in-place more alive than the being,
my father sobbing beside me, the man on the stage
     screaming, the woman behind us starting to
pray,
     the immobilism, the being-in-place more alive than

the being,
     the squad car now faintly visible on the screen
starting the chase up,
     all over my countenance,
the velvet armrest at my fingers, the dollar bill

in my hand,
     choice the thing that wrecks the sensuous here the glorious
                          here—
that wrecks the beauty,
     choice the move that rips the wrappings of light, the
                  ever-tighter wrappings

of the layers of the
     real: what is, what also is, what might be that is,
what could have been that is, what
     might have been that is, what I say that is,
what the words say that is,
     what you imagine the words say that is—Don't move, don't

wreck the shroud, don't move—

AT THE CABARET *NOW*

The Americans are lonely. They don't know what happened.
They're still up and there's all this time yet to kill.
The musicians are still being paid so they keep on.
The sax pants up the ladder, up.
They want to be happy. They want to just let the notes
come on, the mortal wounds, it's all been
paid for so what the hell, each breath going up, up,
them thinking of course Will he make it How far can he
go? Skill, the prince of this kingdom, there at *his* table
now.
Is there some other master, also there, at a
back table, a regular, one we can't make out
but whom the headwaiter knows, the one who never
applauds?
So that it's not about the ending, you see, or where to go
from here.
It's about the breath and how it reaches the trumpeter's hands,
how the hands come so close to touching the breath,
and how the gold thing, gleaming, is there in between,
the only avenue—the long way—captivity.
Like this thing now, slow, extending the metaphor to make a
place. Pledge allegiance. By which is meant
see, here, what a variety tonight, what a good crowd,
some of them saying yes, yes, some others no,
don't they sound good together?
And all around this, space, and seedspores,
and the green continuance.
And all along the musicians still getting paid so let them.
And all around that the motionlessness—
don't think about it though, because you can't.
And then the mother who stayed at home of course because her body . . .
Farewell.
Farewell.
This is the story of a small strict obedience,

human blood.
And how it rivered into all its bloods.
Small stream, really, in the midst of the other ones.
In it children laughing and laughing which is the sound of
ripening.
Which the musicians can't play—but that is another
tale.
Someone invited them in, humanity, and they came in.
They said they knew and then they knew.
They made this bank called justice and then this other one
called not.
They swam in the river although sometimes it was notes.
And some notes are true, even now, yes.
They knew each other, then winter came
which was a curtain, and then spring which was when they realized
it was a curtain.
Which leads us to this, the showstopper: summer, the Americans.
I wish I could tell you the story—so and so holding his glass up,
the table around him jittery,
and how then *she* came along gliding between the tables
whispering *it exists*—enough to drive them all mad of course—
whispering *sharp as salt*, whispering *straw on fire looking at you*—
The Americans whispering it cannot be, stay where you are.
And the one in the back no one knows starting up the applause,
alone,
a flat sound like flesh beating flesh but only *like* it.
Tell me,
why did we live, lord?
Blood in a wind,
why were we meant to live?

FROM THE NEW WORLD

Has to do with the story about the girl who didn't die
    in the gas chamber, who came back out asking
for her mother. Then the moment—the next coil—where the guard,
    Ivan, since the 50's an autoworker in Cleveland,
orders a man on his way in to rape her.
    Then the narrowing, the tightening, but not in hunger, no,—the
                    witness

recollecting this on the stand somewhere in Israel in
    February 87 should You be keeping
track. Has to do with her coming back out? Asking for her mother?
    Can you help me in this?
Are you there in your stillness? Is it a real place?
    God knows I too want the poem to continue,

want the silky swerve into shapeliness
    and then the click shut
and then the issue of sincerity, the glossy diamond-backed
    skin—will you buy me, will you take me home. . . . About the one
who didn't die, her face still there on the new stalk of her body as the
    doors open,

the one who didn't like a relentless treble coming back out
    right here into the thing we call
daylight but which is what now, unmoored?
    The one time I knew something about us
though I couldn't say what

my grandmother then already ill
    took me by the hand asking to be introduced.
And then *no, you are not Jorie—but thank you for*
    saying you are. No. I'm sure. I know her you
see. I went into the bathroom, locked the door.
    Stood in front of the mirrored wall—

not so much to see in, not looking up at all in fact,
     but to be held in it as by a gas,
the thing which was me there in its chamber. Reader,
     they were all in there, I didn't look up,
they were all in there, the coiling and uncoiling
     billions,

the about-to-be-seized,
     the about to be held down,

the about to be held down, bit clean, shaped,
     and the others, too, the ones gone back out, the ending
wrapped round them,
     hands up to their faces why I don't know,

and the about-to-be stepping in,
     one form at a time stepping in as if to stay clean,
stepping over something to get into here,
     something there on the floor now dissolving,
not looking down but stepping up to clear it,

and clearing it,
     stepping in.
Without existence and then with existence.
     Then into the clearing as it clamps down
all round.
     Then into the fable as it clamps down.

     We put her in a Home, mother paid.
We put him in a Home, mother paid.
     There wasn't one that would take both of them we
could afford.
     We were right we put him down the road it's all
there was,
     there was a marriage of fifty years, you know this

already don't you fill in the blanks,

they never saw each other again,
paralyzed on his back the last few years
    he bribed himself a private line, he rigged the phone so he

could talk, etcetera, you know this,
    we put her in X, she'd fallen out we put her back in,
there in her diaper sitting with her purse in her hands all day every
    day, asking can I go now,
meaning him, meaning the
    apartment by then long since let go, you know this

don't you, shifting wind sorting and re-sorting the stuff, flesh,
    now the sunstruck field beyond her window,
now her hands on the forties sunburst silver
    clasp, the white patent-leather pocketbook—
I stood there. Let the silver down all over my shoulders.

    The sink. The goldspeck formica. The water
uncoiling.
    Then the click like a lock being tried.
Then the hollow caressing the back of my neck.
    Then the whole thing like a benediction you can't
shake off,

and the eyes unfastening, nervous, as if they smelled something up there
    and had to go (don't wait for me), the
eyes lifting, up into the decoration, the eyes
    looking. Poor thing.
As if real. As if *in* the place.
    The twitch where the eyes meet the eyes.
A blush.
    You see it's not the matter of her coming back out

alive, is it?
    It's the asking-for. The please.
Isn't it?
    Then the man standing up, the witness, screaming it's him it's him

108

I'm sure your Honor I'm sure. Then Ivan coming up to him
        and Ivan (you saw this) offering his hand, click, whoever
he is, and the old man getting a dial-tone, friend,
        and old whoever clicking and unclicking the clasp, the
silver knobs,
        shall we end on them? a tracking shot? a

close-up on the clasp a two-headed beast it turns out
        made of silvery
leaves? Where would you go now? *Where*
        screaming it's him it's
him? At the point where she comes back out something begins, yes,
        something new, something completely
new, but what—there underneath the screaming—what?

Like what, I wonder, to make the bodies come on, to make
        room,

like what, I whisper,

like which is the last new world, *like, like,* which is the thin

young body (before it's made to go back in) whispering *please.*

UNTITLED

In the city that apparently never was,
where the hero dies and dies to no avail,
where one is not oneself it suddenly appears
(and you, who are you and are you there?)
I found myself at the window at last,
the room inside dark, it being late,
the _____ outside dark, it being night.
Found myself leaning against the pane, the body beneath me
                                                    naked,
and *lateness* not different from *shadow* around me,
and nothing true, nothing distracted into shape around me.

Outside, flashing lights, deep gloom.

A moonless enterprise consisting of towers not there to
        the naked eye.

Consisting of fountains, yes, but invisible, no?
And of what we spoke of in the dead of_____once long ago.
And of long ago.
And of the fountains, too, no?, can't that be true?—
Does it seem to you, too, stranger, that something died?
Something we could call the great *thereness* of being,
the giant,
he who was a wrong idea but was,
the end the singleness like a gazelle could fly into?
See here now how he lies at ease,
the beginning of eternity he lies at ease he did not win
                                                    the day,
his children the points–of–view are dead, they come and go,
have you forgotten?
And that the snow shall not come to unbloom him soon.
Can you feel them on your skin now too,
the layer of lateness and the layer of hurry,

110

and the coating of fear,
and the coating of the theater's empty now, dear, shouldn't we go,
(and then even the voices gone),
and *difference* holding the place in place.
Leaned against the window in the dark
closing my eyes to see that dark,
then opening again to see *that* dark,
opening and shutting to feel them rub against each other in here now
    (only in here),
the shut dark, the open dark—
and in between the _____ where the suspicion of meaning
begins, the suck of shapeliness,
as where this voice narrows now to indicate the nearing
of the end of
the sentence,
and the thin grief called sincerity is born,
and then the city that apparently never was,
the wanting-to-have-really-been, standing up,
standing right up,
and something else (the something else) starting to pool again (all
round) (below) hissing *bend down bend down O wretched wife,*
do you not recognize your love?

THE HIDING PLACE

The last time I saw it was 1968.
Paris, France. The time of the *disturbances*.
We had claims. Schools shut down.
A million *workers* and *students* on strike.

Marches, sit-ins, helicopters, gas.
They stopped you at gunpoint asking for papers.

I spent 11 nights sleeping in the halls. Arguments. *Negotiations*.
Hurrying in the dawn looking for a certain leader
I found his face above an open streetfire.
No he said, tell them *no concessions*.
His voice above the fire as if there were no fire—

language floating everywhere above the sleeping bodies;
and crates of fruit donated in secret;
and torn sheets (for tear gas) tossed down from shuttered windows;
and bread; and blankets, stolen from the firehouse.

The CRS (the government police) would swarm in around dawn
in small blue vans and round us up.
Once I watched the searchbeams play on some flames.
The flames push up into the corridor of light.

In the cell we were so crowded no one could sit or lean.
People peed on each other. I felt a girl
vomiting gently onto my back.
I found two Americans rounded up by chance,
their charter left that morning they screamed, what were they going to
                                                        do?

Later a man in a uniform came in with a stick.
Started beating here and there, found the girl in her eighth month.
He beat her frantically over and over.
He pummeled her belly. Screaming aren't you ashamed?

I remember the cell vividly
but is it from a photograph? I think the shadows as I
　　see them still—the slatted brilliant bits
against the wall—I think they're true—but are they from a photograph?
　　Do I see it from inside now—his hands, her face—or

is it from the new account?
　　The strangest part of getting out again was *streets.*
The light running down them.
　　Everything spilling whenever the wall breaks.
And the air—thick with dwellings—the air filled—doubled—
　　as if the open

had been made to render—
　　The open squeezed for space until the hollows spill out,
story upon story of them
　　starting to light up as I walked out.
How thick was the empty meant to be?
　　What were we finding in the air?

What were we meant to find?
I went home slowly sat in my rented room.
　　Sat for a long time the window open,

　　watched the white gauze curtain sluff this way then that
a bit—
　　watched the air suck it out, push it back in. Lung
of the room with streetcries in it. Watched until the lights
　　outside made it gold, pumping gently.
Was I meant to get up again? I was inside. The century clicked by.
　　The woman below called down *not to forget the*

　　loaf. Crackle of helicopters. Voice on a loudspeaker issuing
warnings.
　　They made agreements we all returned to work.
The government fell but then it was all right again.
　　The man above the fire, listening to my question,

the red wool shirt he wore: where is it? who has it?

He looked straight back into the century: no concessions.
I took the message back.

The look in his eyes—shoving out—into the open—

expressionless with thought:

no—tell them *no*—

THE REGION OF UNLIKENESS

You wake up and you don't know who it is there breathing
　　beside you (the world is a different place from what it
seems)
　　and then you do.
The window is open, it is raining, then it has just
　　ceased. What is the purpose of poetry, friend?
And you, are you one of those girls?
　　The floor which is cold touching your instep now,

is it more alive for those separate instances it crosses
　　up through your whole stalk into your mind?
Five, six times it gets let in, step, step, across to the
　　window.
Then the birdcall tossing quick cuts your way,

a string strung a thousand years ago still taut. . . .
　　He turns in his sleep.
You want to get out of here.
　　The stalls going up in the street below now for market.
Don't wake up. Keep this in black and white. It's

Rome. The man's name . . . ? The speaker
　　thirteen. Walls bare. Light like a dirty towel.
It's *Claudio*. He will overdose before the age of
　　thirty someone told me time
ago. In the bar below, the counterterrorist police

(three of them for this neighborhood) (the Old Ghetto)
　　take coffee. You hear them laugh.
When you lean out you see the butts
　　of the machineguns shake
in the doorway.
　　You wake up from what? Have you been there?
What of this loop called *being* beating against the ends

of things?

    The shutters, as you lean out to push them, creak.
Three boys seen from above run fast down the narrows,
    laughing.
A black dog barks. Was it more than

one night? Was it all right? Where are
    the parents? Dress and get to the door. (Repeat after me).
Now the cold edge of the door crosses her body
    into the field where it will grow. Now the
wrought-iron banister—three floors of it—now the *clack*

clack of her sandals on stone—
    each a new planting—different from all the others—
each planted fast, there, into that soil,
    and the thin strip of light from the heavy street-door,
and the other light after her self has slipped through.
    Later she will walk along and name them, one by

one—the back of the girl in the print dress carrying bread,
    the old woman seen by looking up suddenly.
Later she will walk along, a word in
    each moment, to slap them down onto the plantings,
to keep them still.
    But now it's the hissing of cars passing,

and Left into Campo dei Fiori—
    And though it should be through flames dear god,
it's through clarity,
    through the empty thing with minutes clicking in it,
right through it no resistance,
    running a bit now, the stalls filling all round,
cats in the doorways,
    the woman with artichokes starting it up

—this price then that price—
    right through it, it not burning, not falling, no

piercing sound—
    just the open, day pushing through it, any story pushing through.
Do you want her to go home now? do you want her late for school?
    Here is her empty room,

a trill of light on the white bedspread. This is
    exactly
how slow it moves.
    The women are all in the stalls now.
The one behind the rack of flowers is crying
    —put that in the field for later—into

captivity—
    If I am responsible, it is for what? the field at the
end? the woman weeping in the row of colors? the exact
    shades of color? the actions of the night before?
Is there a way to move through which makes it hard
    enough—thorny, re-

membered? Push. Push through with this girl
    recalled down to the last bit of cartilage, ash, running along the
river now, then down to the bridge, then quick,
    home. Twenty years later

    it's 9:15, I go for a walk, the butterflies are hatching,
(that minute has come),
    and she is still running down the Santo Spirito, and I push her
to go faster, faster, little one, fool, push her, but I'm
    in the field near Tie Siding, the new hatchlings

everywhere—they're drying in the grasses—they lift their wings up
                                     into the
    groundwind—so many—
I kick them gently to make them make room—
    clusters lift with each step—

    and below the women leaning, calling the price out, handling

each fruit, shaking the dirt off. Oh wake up, wake
        up, something moving through the air now, something in the ground
                                                                    that
waits.

HOLY SHROUD

Deadwinter our thornberry
    drags in every last cardinal for miles,
its berries finally
    making it pay.
It's never not this way, the clear promise

drifting without perishing into the empty lots
    where they live,
the stubblefields beyond the mall,
    wafting and almost perishing
into the other stenches desolation and cold
    keep crisp,

garment of signals and truths
    winding itself among us—fronds, dread,
sex and fruit—sour milks and the acids
    of tin—drifting, a prayer that matter
is praying, not really ever
    perishing

unless it's bit by bit into such waiting
    as these birds inhabit,
their readiness where one strain of it
    is finally
heard. Now they're lifting as a large cloth would
    into a corridor of sun,

maybe three hundred sets of lungs
    drifting in unison, showering around this single blade
of sun like so many
    minutes.
Sometimes I watch them
    in the back of

the mall, threading in and out of the discarded
        photobooth, necklacing it, trying
to nest in the plexi face-plate
        someone kicked in
after maybe three thousand faces had leaned
        their images upon it,

unblinking, pressing,
        the one bit of curtain left
flapping into anything's
        voice. But they fold down again now,
down over the whole
        barrenness, limb by bony

limb, seeking the almost invisible stickiness out,
        making it quiver all over unevenly
with their bodyweights and tiny
        leaps, slipping from still to blur between takes
to keep their wiry claws
        unstuck—oh storyline,

down over the whole barrenness—

as when the face which is His,
        which is not our looking,
emerged (the thing not made of human
        glances) (the thing or moment)
during the night of May 23, 18-
        94 and Secondo Pia,

having immersed into the chemical bath
        his last attempt at a clear print
of the holy shroud,
        looked down.
The darkroom hummed.
        The negative image took form.
A face looked out at Pia from

the bottom of the tray,
      a face no one had ever seen before
on the shroud, a face
      that was, he said, unexpected. A face. A thing
whose stare overrides
      the looking. He fainted. The print floated

      to the surface of the surface
where it lives now.
      So that when they pulled the shroud out the front
of the basilica
      and held it up, the archbishop's gold robes
flaring the noonlight
      like an hysteria,

when they held it up laid out lengthwise
      on its frame, a large piece of serge linen
covered with stains and lined with
      red silk,

and it took ten people to hold it,
      staring out into the crowd and squinting up,
the sun pressing against the façade like an interrogation light,
      and down into every beveled cornice,

and down onto the tiny heads and bodies of saints,
      and the tree of life,
and the stone arrows in the stone flesh,
      and Mary on her knees to balance
the composition—When they held it up to us
      we saw nothing, we saw the delay, we saw

the minutes on it, spots here and there,
      we tried to see something, little by little we could almost see,
almost nothing was visible,
      already something other than nothing
was visible in the *almost*.

PICNIC

The light shone down taking the shape of each lie,
    lifting each outline up, making it wear a name.
It was one day near the very end of childhood, Rome,
    out on a field, late April, parents, friends,
after a morning's walk (nearing mid-century),
    some with baskets, some with hats,

(so does it matter that this be true?) some
    picking flowers, meaning by that a door that does not open—
And why should I tell this to you,
    and why should *telling* matter still, the bringing to life of
listening, the party going on down there, grasses,
    voices? Should I tell you who they are, there on the torn

page—should we count them (nine)—and then the girl who
                      was me
    at the edge of the blanket,
two walking off towards what sounds like a stream now?
    Pay attention. Years pass. They are still there.
And the sorrow kept under. And the quick jagged laughs.
    And all the while underneath something else is meant—

the *ladder with no rungs* perhaps, or *things*
    exist?
Meanwhile the wind bends the grasses flat then up again, like that,
    and at the picnic someone's laugh breaks off the mouth
and comes to this.
    Waiting is different from patience, friend. This
is the picnic.
    "Unminding mind, keep in the middle—until" says the silly
                          book where
"Shiva Replies".
    In the field four bluebirds land. *Flish.*
Then no wind for a moment.
    Then someone's laugh, although they are lying,

and X who will sleep with father

later this afternoon.
     The mouths of the gods are stuck open really.
They are sated, exhausted, and still they must devour us.
     After lunch we take a walk.
We walk into their eyes, they cannot stop us,
     we slide on in, a half a dozen human beings
with the day

     off. Their faces are huge.
Back there someone laughs longer than before, too long.
     Click of prongs against a metal bowl.
And you, you have to take this as I
     give it, don't you, eyes, mouth?
Breathe, friend,
     the *sense* here between us must be gotten past, quick,

as any stalk must be gotten past, any body,
     that the hollowness it ferries up slip into here, quick,
using shape as its cover,
     one of me here and one of me there and in between
this thing, watery,
     like a neck rising and craning out

(wanting so to be seen) (as if there were some other place dear god)—.

     When I caught up with them they were down by the pond,
father with X.
     I looked into the water where it was stillest.
Saw how each side wants the other to rip it open.
     Later that day mother came up into the bathroom,
daylight toothy by then,
     color of gunsheen—dusk—

We sat there awhile, neither reached for the switch.
     It was not the thing we call time which was ticking

softly. *Come here* she said gripping my head hard in her hands,
   both of us facing into the mirror.
Then they struck out into the forest one here one there
   wherever they saw it thickest wherever path or track
was absent. As if there were some other place dear god.

   Have you ever looked into standing water and seen it going
very fast,
   seen the breaks in the image where the suction shows,
where the underneath is pointed and its tip shows through,
   maybe something broken, maybe something spoked in there,
your eyes weeds, mouth weeds,
   no bed showing through, no pressure from some shore, no

shore? I looked in there.
   I thought "I should go in". I thought "I want the fate
to come up now, make it come quick, this thing that is
   the predicate"—"is is is is" I thought.
The face stayed there.

   She put her hand out to the glass.
We both stared in—me in the front of her.
   She pulled my hair back very tight.
Took black and started in on the right eye.
   Put it on swiftly. Her hands smelled like wine.
She shadowed the cheek, held the lips open, fixed the
   edge red. She powdered, streaked. I

   never moved. Both of our eyes on the face, on
the third
      party.
Reds, blacks.
   The light started to go we didn't move.
The silver was gone. The edges on things. The face still glowed—

bright in the wetness, there.
   Why should the shut thing not be true enough

124

anymore?
  (Open up open open the stillness shrieked.)
Why do we *think*? What is the thinking for?
  When Psyche met the god he came down to her

  through the opening which is *waiting*,
the *not living* you can keep alive in you,
  the god in the house. We painted that alive,
mother with her hands
  fixing the outline clear—eyeholes, mouthhole—
forcing the expression on.
  Until it was the only thing in the end of the day that seemed

believable,
  and the issue of candor coming awake, there,
one face behind the other peering in,
  and the issue of
freedom. . . .
  Outside it's almost spring in earnest. The Princess

known as *Luciana*
  back from the picnic
has spent one afternoon of light on the lawn tweezing hair
  from her legs. More drinks. The women talk.
Should she marry the arms merchant named Rudi?
  Is hisses the last light on the reddish berries, *is is* the much

blacker shadows of spring now that the leaves are
  opening, now that they're taking up

place.

CHAOS

(EVE)

1

What is it shall be torn off and held up, hanging—skin
    with a face in the folds of it—for
judgment?
    Here is the skin of days in the one hand of God,
drooping, the face running like ink in rain.
    Devils jump away frightened.
Nothing scarier.
    Animals flee. The skin of *days.*

    Here is the skin of *waiting.* The animals turn back,
they can smell it. It stinks with its silly smile. Hands still on
    the long strips of skin;
eyeholes.

    Here is the skin of having been touched.
Where the fingers of others ran—stitchmarks, bleeding.
    The soles of the feet red
where the earth leaned on them, where it forced them to
    still it.
Where the fingers of others have been: rips,
    blood even though it's empty, riffs.

The skin made of the looks of others held up at the end of a long fork,
    then cast into the pit, the open eye of
the one God (the Devils can watch now)
    (the animals can watch) . . . What will He piece them into,
hundreds lifted up at a glance, some
    with the feet still on,

the waters rising up for a look,

126

the fires ripped up to see shape begin—
this foot then that fold—strips sewn back together—
    air bending down to see the sharp new line,
where the inside begins to be sealed off,
        where the stitchwork is tucked under,
soil swaying up in a wall to see choices

        begin—an elbow, one mouth—
the bat-winged angels hiding their faces but watching,
    the waters rising, the Finishing beginning now, the garment which
                                        is closed,
by which the open is enhanced, by which the open
        is freed—.
The air rises up.
    The fire burns further.
The open, the open.
    Then the knot is pulled in, the outline, the

judgment.
    Then He puts it down on the soil, the thing made of skins,
its hands resting one
        on the earth, one on the thigh. The head back. The hum,
can you hear it,
        beginning. And the thing still inside him, the girl,

still there inside him, awake,
        wearing him tight all round her like this,
him sealed, breathing,
        her inside his sleeping now, inside the minutes, inside them.

                            2

    Then there's the time the elevator stopped for some
reason,
        her in there with me, old woman,
deep in the heart of the building,

someplace daylight has never been.

We didn't speak.
　　We stayed there a while like that.
I pushed down. Pushed *open*.
　　She wandered all night by then. Hid certain things—whisk,
radio antenna.
　　After a while I found the path she took
by the wear in the rug—

a figure eight—
　　one wing more pronounced where it wrapped all night
round the recliner he'd
　　fall asleep in.
The TV hummed.
　　For a while after them there was wind through there.
I went by for some reason,

door not even locked,
　　walls bare, floors bare—a window open.
It stood empty for a long time then someone else took it.
　　The other wing
wove round the low table with all the wrapped candy—
　　Here have some, have some, gesturing towards our bodies—

I tried all the buttons—two unmarked ones.
　　She started in on the names of
ours,
　　the dead ones, the other ones,

　　the whole chain down.
There seemed to be no one to call.
　　I thought of how much air we had.
The names came gently,
　　almost one with the breath,

　　though they stuck to the top of it, they took its way

out, fast to the heat of it, syllable, syllable. . . .
　　　Then she pushed her hand down onto my arm.
Then she gripped down hard.
　　　The list didn't slow, where was I, was she starting over

or did it just seem that way?
　　　She'd sit in the office all day while he worked, very still,
　　　　　　　　　　　　　　　　　　　　　smoking,
for thirty-five years,
　　　sometimes me in the corner,
the spike-headed minutes pushing up round her,
　　　up under the thighs, there at the elbows, the hips,

　　　sat in the day like the day,
only the wrist moving really,
　　　cigarette, two barely split fingers, the bone in them—
Behind the wall the men at work—
　　　saws, stitching machines, the dry sound of skins
being cut—

　　　and the mink that are sliced into ¼-inch strips,
and the matcher with his monocle,
　　　and how you have to make the skins of hundreds seem it's all

one animal—Further back there's the icebox,
　　　there's beaver musk marten fisher,
ermine silverfox bluefox redfox,
　　　bear wolf weasel wildcat otter, sable and lynx,
wolverine, lamb—
　　　In the mirror-room,

　　　there's the spot where you're thousands going endlessly in,
there's the spot where you're one,
　　　there's the spot where you can't be found—
Why should it come alive, the thing inside, who said it had

to come alive?
Click of the lighter.

    Traffic way down there. The six a.m. train, the six p.m. train.
Not even the foot on her crossed leg moved.

    Try not to make noise,

    try not to make noise that will call them all in,
her look going out from her into the office,

    her look pouring out from her, nothing going back in,
one way sweetheart, here have some, have some more,

    sometimes a hand into the bottom drawer for a new pack
darting.

3

    Because the hole that opens in him is the edge of matter,
the very edge,

    the sensation of there not being enough
—that rip—and then the squinting to see

    —what is it out there?—
out of which the taut beast begins to grow,

    and rapidly, the sensation of lateness pulling up out of

    the sensation of there not being
enough

    (as you up out of this now pull)—
rising up out of the gloam

    like a name being called—
Who knew we needed anyone?

    Once I watched at the kitchen window a long time

as something rose out of the end of night,

    out of the roiling darks rising and wafting over the still darks,
until folds appeared,

    and folds in those folds,
and tucks where darkness stayed, held,

    and large loose cloths of it which the wind saw and dropped

130

down to—
    Until some shadows were hidden (and *underneaths* began),
until some cast up twisting (greens?),
    until some fell back after being used, thinner now—dusts,
silts—
    and the blossoming white hawthorne rose out of the very end of night.
The earth turned.
    The earth spit it forth.

There's the god that locked herself in the tower, there's the
    one cast out into the hissing open,
the white pushing out,
    the white flaring and pushing,
until the whole thing steps out, opening and shuddering, thousands

of wings,
    into the early morning, into the late twentieth century.
I stood there.
    There was a hole in my head where the thing stepped in.
The hole grew wider.
    Limbs on all sides pushed away from the center.
Depth started to throb.
    The hole in my head ripped a bit wider.
Now there were acrid smells. Greens. Degrees.
    Something all round stepping back, away.

    The tree rose into sight. Stayed.
The question of the place of origin is not true, too slow.
    Love pushed out into the watching brain.
Everything changed, stilled.
    I say *please* and then you are real.
The shape took hold.
    Stepped free.
And yes it was a poorer land then.
    Birds everywhere. Chatter in the upper branches.

THE MARRIAGE

1

I'm taking the ashes from the woodstove out.
Some for the flowerbed? Some for the garden?
They float off my hand, it's snowing on the mountain.
"Whose green mind bulges under the complicated hues?"
I hardly even need to toss them now.
As if there were another wind, there at the edge of matter,
they float, they lean on something I can't find, they follow it,
skipping over what's too slow, there now beneath them,
earth.
A moth is fascinated, come closer.
Come, come, the trouble will not stop, pay attention.
It's snowing on the mountain.
And what are these the ash *of*, please?
Of what was shouted out between axestrokes (the text)?
Of the scent where dogwood had begun to open here and there
between the pine?
(*Vladimir and Estragon begin to cry*)
Of the hand lifted to shade the eyes
raised now to gauge
the height (*They do not move*) and is it dead all the way
up? (*They do not move*).
You look at something and then you look and then the body perishes.
(*They do not move*).
In E's painting it's the end of the party, dusk, the bride
still in her white is sitting in the green lawnchair,
cigarette in one hand, drink in the other,
crossed leg still swinging now a
spangly shoe.
Off to the left a small dog sniffs.
I suppose she might as well get up, don't you?
She might as well, no one is looking really,
here in the vague sweet chanciness,

she might as well, it's dark enough, voices spread round
that will not, ever, be
returned to earth—
the leak's only one way—
as the smell of dogwood now just opening will not,
or the actual shades of green that hawk
around, penumbral, that spread a bit, that do not set sail—no, not
today—
or the twenty-four hours that will not be returned, ever—
And would she tell him, really, if she could—
could it be taken *in*?—pitterpatter now as Flesh goes by—

2

Later it will be the world as it has become.
Everyone will have waved adieu, there will be just the two of them.
The hum will be the car.
And the night all round them, bristling,
and the silver bits of them now floating through . . .
It will be the world as we know it—When she comes down
he will be asleep drunk in the TV
hum.
Were you expecting the queen to reappear?
It is *relaxed as dirt*
this barrenness become a place—
Her dress. What should she do with it? And she hears other
hums—freezer, two different clocks—words will come later on (it's
snowing on the mountain) something to live against will come.
For now it's a matter of whether to cover him or let him
grow cold there.
Whether to switch the channels off or let the hum stay with him
there.
Whether to wake him and say words and feel the year
clot.
What should the poem do?
What can still be

saved?

No hint had been given her, there halfway down the stairs,

having come look for him, hand groping the lightswitch,

seeing the world there in its blue light,

her still in her dress,

and offshore, way offshore,

arm rising in surprise to the mouth now (or so it seems from here)—

no hint

whether to waken him whether to leave him there the icon the

chosen one the only reader in his shadowless

desire to be the end that will not end—

And so it was to be (I could tell her) night after night

(am I allowed to tell her?) asleep in his sleep in the hum.

Come closer. You look at something and then you

look. She floats off my hand.

Wind takes her for no reason for

a while.

Coo coo says the dove, gray-blue, floating up out of nowhere, pay

attention.

(*Well, shall we go?*)

(*Yes, yes let's go*)

(*They do not move*)

Softly she sang a bit then went upstairs.

THE TREE OF KNOWLEDGE

Then I came down and watched the fire awhile.
The marriage hymn, the star-spangled fire.
  There was a flame that seemed a bluegreen claw
at the end of a sawed-off length of limb,
    —a fingery, pointing, grabbing thing
pushing right up out of the body it charred,

  all the mad reds fetched-up with whites around it,
swarming, bubbling.
  No longer any of the inhale-exhale you get in a fire,
long past the flash and excitement, no
    desire,
just this insistent thing, much hotter, at its
    apogee—hollow—quick—

  just appearance turning into further appearance,
click.
  I watched the claw a long time.
Tried not to see it as reaching. Tried not to see it
    as pointing, as being
released.
  Have you ever wanted to put your hand right in,

  to open it up and push it deep in there,
to make the *other thing* begin?
  Meanwhile the marquee all studded up with fear, buzzing,
blazing,
    me waiting underneath in the parked car for the one hour
you took karate class, the girls smeared
    into the one good piece of shade

at the frontier pawnshop and incandescent ticket booth,
    the red and ice-white neon strobe blinking over the whole
truth
    making us come and go like

dice being tossed.

   Now it's up—how much are we worth?
What does He want, what does He need

   to win this one, old man poking the fire, making it
air-up right, making the coals flame up.

   He turns back to the game.
See Him?

   He's got some kind of diagram.
I'm parked at x. You're in the storefront at y.

   It's winter so it's dark early and from out here we can really

                                          see you

behind the glass all lit up now and flat flat,

   nine rows of boys all raising one arm up
and thrusting it forward

   hard with a jump,
the cry that's forced up out of your lungs

   lost to the glass

   so you look lacquered, gold, mouths open wide, kicking in rows—
Do you embarrass us?

   The girls are to the left of you—The classroom's light
making gold rows on the sidewalk they can be bought

   out of—Mixed with the strobe,
mixed with the short in the marquee,

it makes the clot of us

   bubble, glitter—icy—
with whatever it is that must be given up,

   exalted or spit up, frothing,
coming to boil—they turn, they turn back, one stops

   to shout, a cigarette, hope, armload of

spangles, charms,

   all the wattage of the marquee for a flash on the comb
in her hair, on the chain round

136

her thigh. No sky.
I kept the car locked.
        Class took less than an hour.
Here you are now in your suit as before,

        the briefcase with clothes in it, the belt of some rank.
What can you kill?
        You told me once driving home—
how frail the bones are at the neck,
        how still you have to be to find them in the wreck of
intervening flesh,
        how rage must not come into

play,
        how cool the gesture keeps you when precise,
how then you can see behind
        yourself,
how then you can hear the other man's mind.
        The edge of your hand—you held it up at a traffic light—

was enough—
        People walked by in front of the car.
The cross-street hummed.
        Steak signs bristled on and off.
The map of the city shined and shined.

        Can you read it now, Transparency?
Is this Your round?
        Can You see them in there now, behind the marquee, the rows
                                                of heads
with hands attached, a sob here and there, some with
        their hats still on. A hiss. See us?
Hear the slapping sound of flesh on

flesh? The bits of face lit up—eye here, a socket, a
        lip? Onstage a girl
is alone on the bed,
        knees bulging up, elbows,
the head up now then down, the hand

sometimes in view then gone, a pillow I
believe—a queen size bed—one light above—the red

get-up she's wearing stretched on tight,
    the rear-end up, shimmering, what light there is on it, red silk,
                                        a shout
from the dark, a soft dry shout.
    When I reached for your hand in there,
when I ran my hand onto your hand,
    it was to get that other sense of flesh,

where touch is the way to disappear,
    the old dream of an underneath,
is it still there?
    I feel the very top of your hand.
I feel the edge of you, the souvenir.
    Ruffle the skin—gently.
Look down at it. Then close my eyes. Then try again.
    What if there is no other side to this anymore—

just skin, skin,
    rippling, folding under, tucked tight, taking
shape—rounding the corners, lining the
    singleness, opening here and there to let the
eye through—
    the sound of a moan now but magnified,

the sound of a moan in the speakers—
    the red velvet corridors leafing back that way,
ticket booths, concession stands—brocade, embossed organza—
    gold trimming, recessed lighting, rooms, rest rooms,
back that way, branching back, all the red foliage,
    more in every direction,
starting from this plush armrest
    with the reddish hand splayed out on it I can
no longer feel

    out to the four edges of the only known world.

138

SHORT HISTORY OF THE WEST

Tap tap.
    A blue sky. A sun and moon in it.
Peel it back.
    The angels in ranks, the *about.*
Peel it back.
    Tap tap the underneath.
Blood where the sky has opened.
    And numbers in there—god how they sing—tap tap—

and the little hammer underneath,
    and a hand holding the lid true.
What are you building little man?
    What's it like, what's it for?
We're going now, you stay in there.
    Deep in, nail at a time.
We're putting this back down, down over you, you stay in there,
    and then the storyline which starts where the gold doors

fold over the grassy curtain, click,
    and then the *and so*—hair falling
down all over—and the sky on now and the red sun on and the sunbeam,
    and the thing at the end of its reach—the girl
in the room down there, at her kitchen table,
    the last pool of light on her plate,

and how you must think of her now—tired, or free,
    or full of *feeling*—and the light she should rise
to switch on now,
    and how she will not rise.

WHAT IS CALLED THINKING

When I surprised the deer the wind was against me.
So I was given a length
  of naive time, green time, free,
to be the sole
  witness,
her blinking in and out of the one ray of light
  sorting tufts,
me in the Walkman where the self-reflexive strings of the
             eighteenth century

do not die down.
  I stood there, fast.
Wanted the arabesques of strings, the nervousness, to brand
            themselves hard,
  onto her intangible
pelt. Watched the skin ripple
  to rid itself of flies. And the ray lacerate
the broad soft back
  to its infinite pleasure,

and her take a short step through.
  Up in the air, in the transparent unmoving frenzy, the mind,
oars beat softly in time.
  A head sank into the gutter (blood starting out).
The strings interpreted (the wind stayed against me).
  Mother bent to light the candles.
Flight of a bluejay like a struck
  match.
Then twenty abreast (click) (click).
  Then twenty abreast marching through the city—

and all along the strings, the strings, bawdy, winged,
  (trying to make sure it's a *story* after
all) . . .

Barehanded they grip the oars.
The lower limb of the aspen shakes.
       She looks up—it is a she?—
and there is the angel sitting on the limb now.
       There is the angel laughing, sharpening blades.
There is the angel—its robes the *mistakes*

       slapping the taller grasses; its sharpening (the *good
ideas*)—forwards, forwards, forwards, forwards.
       She goes back to feeding, the angel is on her.
He is grinning and slicing the air all round him.
       He is testing the blade (the air is blue).
When I look again it's an AK-47 then it's a saber.
       Look it's a spinning wheel, a printing press—no

it's a run of celluloid in his right hand—he's waving it—
       it's 78 frames of some story—then it's the simple
blade again.
       How can the deer let him ride her?
The *click* is my tape going into
       reverse play. The oboe. The *thinking it's for*

something—that sadness—
       sluffing over the god: tree deer blade:
is it going to braid them up right this time—the good
       elegy—the being
so sorry?
       If I could whip her with the strings,

       if I could stab her with the rising sound of
violins—
       but the oars continue above us—we are so small—
and the angel is floating,
       and the angel is knifing himself
to make the laughter flow
       (although it's breeze-rustle in the honeyed aspen),
over and over the long blade

            going into the windy robes,
sometimes crossing through sometimes staying inside awhile,
        sometimes straight through the throat, then up the nose,
his foliate windiness laughing,
        lacerating the stillness with the silent laughter
(as the breeze picks up down to the left)
        (and she looks up, peering out) and the wind

        begins to change her way,
the angel wild now on the grasses,
        the tree above her wholly hung with knives—hundreds—
                                    clacking—

until I want them all to
        fall on her at once—dozens,
into the lowered neck, the saddle—
        the wind changing round altogether now—
until he gives it to me—the good angel—since I
        thought of it: and she turns to

me here now,
        and all the blades fall suddenly
into all parts of me giving me my
        human
shape.

History!
        A dress rustles on the spiral staircase.
I lay my forehead into the silver hands.

ACT III, SC. 2

Look she said this is not the distance
we wanted to stay at—We wanted to get
close, very close. But what
is the way in again? And is it

too late? She could hear the actions
rushing past—but they are on
another track. And in the silence,
or whatever it is that follows,

there was still the buzzing: motes, spores,
aftereffects and whatnot recalled the morning after.
Then the thickness you can't get past called *waiting*.

Then the you, whoever you are, peering down to see if it's
                                                    done yet.
Then just the look on things of being looked-at.
Then just the look on things of being seen.

HISTORY

    So that I had to look up just now to see them
sinking—black storks—
    sky disappearing as they ease down,
each body like a prey the wings have seized . . .
    Something that was a *whole story* once,
unparaphrased by shadow,

    something that was the whole cloth floating in a wide
sky,
    rippling, studded with wingbeats,
something like light grazing on the back of light,

    now getting sucked back down
into the watching eye, flapping, black
    hysterical applause,
claws out now looking for foothold,
    high-pitched shrieks,

then many black lowerings—dozens—
    shadowing the empty limbs, the ground,
tripling the shadowload . . .
    Look up and something's unwrapping—
Look up and it's suitors, applause,
    it's fast-forward into the labyrinth,

    smell of ammonia,
lassitude,
    till finally they're settling, shadows of shadows, over
                       the crown, in every
requisite spot.
    Knowledge.
They sit there. Ruffling. The tree is black.
    Should I move? Perhaps they have forgotten me.
Perhaps it is *absolutely true* this thing in the tree

above me?
　　Perhaps as they hang on hang on it is *the afternoon*?
Voice of what. Seems to say what.
　　This is newness? This is the messenger? Screeching.
Clucking.

　　Under the frozen river the other river flows
on its side in the dark
　　now that it cannot take into itself
the faces, the eyes—the gleam in them—the tossed-up hand
　　pointing then casting the pebble

in.
　　Forget what we used to be, doubled, in the dark
age where half of us is cast
　　in and down, all the way,
into the silt,
　　roiled under,

saved in there with all the other slaughtered bits,
　　dark thick fabric of the underneath,
sinking, sifting.
　　It is four o'clock. I have an appointment.
The tree above me. The river not flowing. Now:

feel the creature, the x:
　　me notched into place here,
the grassy riverbank and every individual stem,
　　the stalks and seedheads rattling at waterline,

the river made of the eyes of beavers, otters,
　　of everything inside watching and listening,
the dredger parked in the river-house,
　　the slap slap and click inside the water
the water swallows,

my looking-up, the spine of

the x—the supple, beastly
spine.
    As long as I stand here, as long as I can stay still,
the x is alive.
    Being here and then the feeling of being. . . .

Everything has its moment.
    The x gnaws on its bone.
When it's time it will know.
    Some part of it bleats, some part of it is
the front, has a face,

when it's time it will be time.
    God it is in no hurry, there is no hurry.
It gnaws on the bone making minutes.
    Let's *move*
—but it does not move—
    When it's time it will be done,
but it is not time.
    I who used to be inconsolable (and the world

wild around me)
    can stand here now.
It's not that I am alone or that you are or why—
    It's not that we are watched-over or that the x's back
is turned.
    No.
It's that we've grown—
    it's that one must grow—consolable. Listen:
the x gnaws, making stories like small smacking

sounds,
    whole long stories which are its gentle gnawing.
Sometimes it turns onto its side.
    It takes its time.
Let it be so. Shame. Drops of light.
    If the x is on a chain, licking its bone,

making the sounds now of monks
       copying the texts out,
muttering to themselves,
       if it is on a chain
(the lights snapping on now all along the river)
       if it is on a chain

that hisses as it moves with the moving x,
       link by link with the turning x
(the gnawing now Europe burning)
       (the delicate chewing where the atom splits),
if it is on a chain—
       even this beast—even this the favorite beast—
then this is the chain, the gleaming

       chain: that what I wanted was to have looked up at the right
time,
       to see what I was meant to see,
to be pried up out of my immortal soul,
       up, into the sizzling quick—

That what I wanted was to have looked up at the only
       right time, the intended time,
punctual,
       the millisecond I was bred to look up into, click, no
half-tone, no orchard of
       possibilities,

up into the eyes of my own
       fate not the world's.
The bough still shakes.

THE PHASE AFTER HISTORY

1

Then two juncos trapped in the house this morning.
   The house like a head with nothing inside.
The voice says: come in.
   The voice always whispering *come in, come.*
Stuck on its one track.
   As if there were only one track.

Only one way in.
   Only one *in.*
The house like a head with nothing inside.
   A table in the white room.
Scissors on the table.
   Two juncos flying desperately around the
room of the house like a head
   (with nothing inside)
the voice-over keeping on (come in, *in*),
   them fizzing around the diagram that makes no

   sense—garden of upstairs and downstairs—wilderness
of materialized
   meaning.
Home.
   Like this piece of paper—
yes take this piece of paper—
   the map of the house like a head with
whatever inside—two birds—

   and on it all my efforts to get the *house* out of their
way—
   to make detail withdraw its hot hand,
its competing naturalness—
   Then I open the two doors to make a draft

(here)—
     meaning by that an imbalance

     for them to find and ride—
The inaudible hiss—justice—washing through,
     the white sentence that comes alive to
rectify imbalance—
     —give me a minute.
In the meantime

     they fly into the panes of glass: bright light,
silently they throw themselves into its law: bright light,
     they float past dreamed-up on the screen
called 7 a.m., nesting season, black blurry terms,
     the thwacking of their
heads onto resistant
     surfaces.
Then one escapes,

sucked out by the doorful of sky,
     the insanity, *elsewhere*,
so that—give me a second—
     I no longer remember it,
and the other one vanishes though into here, upstairs,
     the voice still hissing under the track *in in*,

the voice still hissing over the track.
     What you do now is wait
for the sound of wings to be heard
     somewhere in the house
—the *peep* as of glass bottles clinking,
     the lisp of a left-open book read by breeze,
or a hand going into the pile of dead leaves—

(as where there is no *in*, therefore)
     (as where—give me a minute—someone laughs upstairs
but it's really wings

                rustling up there
on the cold current called history
            which means of course it's late and I've
got things

to do).
            How late is it: for instance, is this a sign?
Two birds then one: is it a meaning?
        I start with the attic, moving down.
Once I find it in the guest-
            bedroom but can't
catch it in time,
            talking to it all along, hissing: stay there, don't

move—absolutely no
        story—sure there is a sound I could make with my throat
and its cupful of wind that could transmit
        meaning. Still I say sharply as I move towards it hands out—
High-pitched the sound it makes with its throat,
        low and too tender the sound it makes with its

        body—against the walls now,
down.
        Which America is it in?
Which America are we in here?
        Is there an America comprised wholly
of its waiting and my waiting and all forms of the thing

even the green's—
        a large uncut fabric floating above the soil—
a place of *attention*?
        The voice says wait. Taking a lot of words.
The voice always says wait.
        The sentence like a tongue
in a higher mouth
        to make the other utterance, the inaudible one,
possible,

150

the sentence in its hole, its cavity
of listening,
    flapping, half dead on the wing, through the
hollow indoors,
    the house like a head
with nothing inside
    except this breeze—
shall we keep going?
    Where is it, in the century clicking by?
Where, in the America that *exists*?
    This castle hath a pleasant seat,

the air nimbly recommends itself,
    the guest approves
by his beloved mansionry
    that heaven's breath smells wooingly here.

2

    The police came and got Stuart, brought him to
Psych Hospital.
    The face on him the face he'd tried to cut off.
Starting at the edge where the hair is fastened.
    Down behind the ear.
As if to lift it off and give it back. Easy. Something
    gelatinous,
an exterior
    destroyed by mismanagement.

Nonetheless it stayed on.
    You suffer and find the outline, the right
seam (what the suffering is for)—
    you find *where it comes off*: why can't it come off?
The police brought him to Admitting and he can
    be found there.

Who would have imagined a face
  could be so full of blood.

Later he can be found in a room on *four*.
  He looks up when you walk in but not at yours.
Hope is something which lies flat against the wall,
  a bad paint job, peeling in spots.
Some people move by in the hallway,

  some are referred elsewhere or they
wait.
  There is a transaction going on up ahead, a commotion.
Shelley is screaming again about the Queen.
  There is a draft here but between two unseen
openings.
  And there is the Western God afraid His face would come off
into our eyes
  so that we have to wait in the cleft
rock—remember?—
  His hand still down on it, we're waiting for Him to
go by,

  the back of Him is hope, remember,
the off-white wall,
  the thing-in-us-which-is-a-kind-of-fire fluttering
as we wait in here
  for His hand to lift off,
the thing-in-us-which-is-a-kind-of-air
  getting coated with waiting, with the cold satinfinish,

the thing-which-trails-behind (I dare do all that may
  become a man,
who dares do more is none)
  getting coated, thickly. Oh screw thy story to the
sticking place—
  When he looks up

152

because he has had the electric shock,
and maybe even the insulin shock we're not sure,

the face is gone.
It's hiding somewhere in here now.
I look and there's no listening in it, foggy place.
We called him the little twinkler
says his mother at the commitment hearing,

because he was the happiest.
The blood in the upstairs of the duplex getting cold.
Then we have to get the car unimpounded.
Send the keys to his parents.
Do they want the car?
His wrists tied down to the sides of the bed.
And the face on that shouldn't come off.
The face on that mustn't come off.
Scars all round it along the hairline under the
chin.
Later he had to take the whole body off

to get the face.
But me in there while he was still breathing,
both of us waiting to hear something rustle
and get to it
before it rammed its lights out
aiming for the brightest spot, the only clue.

3

Because it is the face
which must be taken off—?
the forward-pointing of it, history?
that we be returned to the faceless
attention,

153

the waiting and waiting for the telling sound.
Am I alone here?
Did it get out when the other one did
and I miss it?
Tomorrow and tomorrow and tomorrow.
The head empty, yes,

but on it the face, the idea of principal witness,
the long corridor behind it—
a garden at one end and a garden at
the other—
the spot of the face
on the expanse of the body,
the spot on the emptiness (tomorrow and tomorrow),
the spot pointing
into every direction, looking, trying to find
corners—

(and all along the cloth of Being fluttering)
(and all along the cloth, the sleep—
before the beginning, before the itch—)
How I would get it back,
sitting here on the second-floor landing,
one flight above me one flight below,
listening for the one notch
on the listening which isn't me

listening—
Sleep, sleep, but on it the dream of reason, eyed,
pointing forward, tapering for entry,
the *look* with its meeting place at
vanishing point, blade honed for
quick entry,
etcetera, glance, glance again,
(make my keen knife see not the
wound it makes)—
So that you 1) must kill the King—yes—
2) must let her change, change—until you lose her,

154

the creature made of nets,
  whose eyes are closed,
whose left hand is raised
  (now now now now hisses the voice)
(her hair made of sentences) and
  3) something new come in but
what? listening.
  Is the house empty?
Is the emptiness housed?
  Where is America here from the landing, my face on

my knees, eyes closed to hear
  further?
Lady M. is the intermediary phase.
  God help us.
Unsexed unmanned.
  Her open hand like a verb slowly descending onto
                                        the free,
her open hand fluttering all round her face now,
  trying to still her gaze, to snag it on

those white hands waving and diving
  in the water that is not there.

SOUL SAYS

(AFTERWORD)

To be so held by brittleness, shapeliness.
By meaning. As where I *have to go where you go,*
I *have to touch what you must touch,*
in hunger, in boredom, the spindrift, the ticket . . .
Distilled in you (can you hear me)
the idiom in you, the why—

The flash *of a voice.* The river *glints.*
The mother *opens the tablecloth up into the wind.*
There as the fabric descends—the alphabet of ripenesses,
what is, what could have been.
The bread on the tablecloth. Crickets shrill in the grass.

O pluck my magic garment from me. So.
                              [lays down his robe]
Lie there, my art—

(This is a form of matter of matter she sang)

(Where the hurry is stopped) (and held) (but not extinguished) (no)

(So listen, listen, this will soothe you) (if that is what you want)

Now then, I said, I go to meet that which I liken to
(even though the wave break and drown me in laughter)
the wave breaking, the wave drowning me in laughter—

from

MATERIALISM

Notes on the Reality of the Self

Watching the river, each handful of it closing over the next,
brown and swollen. Oaklimbs,
gnawed at by waterfilm, lifted, relifted, lapped-at all day in
this dance of non-discovery. All things are
possible. Last year's leaves, coming unstuck from shore,
rippling suddenly again with the illusion,
and carried, twirling, shiny again and fat,
towards the quick throes of another tentative
conclusion, bobbing, circling in little suctions their stiff
                                        presence
on the surface compels. Nothing is virtual.
The long brown throat of it sucking up from some faraway melt.
Expression pouring forth, all content no meaning.
The force of it and the thingness of it identical.
Spit forth, licked up, snapped where the force
exceeds the weight, clickings, pockets.
A long sigh through the land, an exhalation.
I let the dog loose in this stretch. Crocus
appear in the gassy dank leaves. Many
earth gasses, rot gasses.
I take them in, breath at a time, I put my
breath back out
onto the scented immaterial. How the invisible
roils. I see it from here and then
I see it from here. Is there a new way of looking—
valences and little hooks—inevitabilities, proba-
bilities? It flaps and slaps. Is this body the one
I know as me? How private these words? And these? Can you
smell it, brown with little froths at the rot's lips,
meanwhiles and meanwhiles thawing then growing soggy then
the filaments where leaf-matter accrued round a
pattern, a law, slipping off, precariously, bit by bit,

159

and flicks, and swiftnesses suddenly more water than not.
The nature of goodness the mind exhales.
I see myself. I am a widening angle of
and *nevertheless* and *this performance has rapidly*—
nailing each point and then each next right point, inter-
locking, correct, correct again, each rightness snapping loose,
floating, hook in the air, swirling, seed-down,
quick—*the evidence of the visual henceforth*—and henceforth, loosening—

STEERING WHEEL

In the rear-view mirror I saw the veil of leaves
suctioned up by a change in current
and how they stayed up, for the allotted time,
in absolute fidelity to the force behind,
magenta, hovering, a thing that happens,
slowly upswirling above the driveway
I was preparing to back clear out of—
and three young pine trees at the end of that view
as if aghast with bristling stillness—
and the soft red updraft without hesitation
aswirl in their prickly enclosing midst—
and on the radio I bent to press on,
a section with rising strings plugging in,
crisp with distinctions, of the earlier order.
Oh but I haven't gotten it right.
You couldn't say that it was matter.
I couldn't say that it was sadness.
Then a hat from someone down the block
blown off, rolling—tossing—across the empty macadam,
an open mouth, with no face round it,
O and O and O and O—
"we have to regain the moral pleasure
of experiencing the distance between subject and object,"
—me now slowly backing up
the dusty driveway into the law
composed of updraft, downdraft, weight of these dried
                                    midwinter leaves,
light figured-in too, I'm sure, the weight of light,
and angle of vision, dust, gravity, solitude,
and the part of the law which is the world's waiting,
and the part of the law which is my waiting,
and then the part which is my impatience—now; *now?*—

though there are, there really are,
things in the world, you must believe me.

Notes on the Reality of the Self

In my bushes facing the bandpractice field,
in the last light, surrounded by drumbeats, drumrolls,
there is a wind that tips the reddish leaves
exactly all one way, seizing them up from underneath, making them
barbarous in unison. Meanwhile the light insists they glow
where the wind churns, or no, there is a wide gold corridor
of thick insistent light, layered with golds, as if runged,
as if laid low from the edge of the sky,
in and out of which the coupling and uncoupling
limbs—the racks of limbs—the luminosities of branchings—
offspring and more offspring—roil—(except when a sudden
                                   stillness reveals
an appall of pure form, pure light—
every rim clear, every leaf serrated, tongued—stripped
of the gauzy quicknesses which seemed its flesh)—but then
                                   the instabilities
regroup, and the upper limbs of the tall oaks
begin to whine again with wide slappings
which seep ever-downward to my bushes—into them, through them—
to where the very grass makes congress with the busyness—
mutating, ridging, threshing this light from that, to no
avail—and in it all
the drumroll, rising as the ranks join in,
the wild branches letting the even drumbeats through,
ripples let through as the red branches spiral, tease,
as the crescendos of the single master-drummer
rise, and birds scatter over the field, and the wind makes each
                                   thing
kneel and rise, kneel and rise, never-ending stringy
almost maternal lurching of wind
pushing into and out of the russets, magentas, incarnadines . . .
Tell me, where are the drumbeats which fully load and expand
                                   each second,

bloating it up, cell-like, making it real, where are they
to go, what will *they* fill up
pouring forth, pouring round the subaqueous magenta bushes
which dagger the wind back down on itself,
tenderly, prudently, almost loaded down
with regret? For there is not a sound the bushes will take
from the multitude beyond them, in the field, uniformed—
(all left now on one heel) (right) (all fifty trumpets up
to the sun)—not a molecule of sound
from the tactics of this glistening beast,
forelimbs of silver (trombones, french horns)
(anointed by the day itself) expanding, retracting,
bits of red from the surrounding foliage deep
                    in all the fulgid
instruments—orient—ablaze where the sound is released—
trumpeting, unfolding—
                            screeching, rolling, patterning, measuring—
scintillant beast the bushes do not know exists
as the wind beats them, beats in them, beats round them,
them in a wind that does not really even now
                            exist,
in which these knobby reddish limbs that do not sway
                    by so much as an inch
its arctic course
                    themselves now sway—

RELATIVITY: A QUARTET

1

During the slowdown we lost power
    along the northeast corridor—it taking a moment before I
                                      realized
we were at a crawl, then the slow
               catch,
    and we were still. I heard the cars behind me each
receive the jolt
    of stillness.
Felt the transfer of

inertia
    slither through,
creaking,
    then an aftershock—
long the backbone.
    Nothing shrill. A hiss clenched it.

    Across the aisle a girl and her father woke, looked out.
Monologue of going and going interrupted.
    The land looked truant, incomplete. On their side, through
                                   trees,
the ocean looked too pressed with
    definition? incomparability? what is it that leaks
                    out of it, *scene,*
once it's the untheoretical *here*—sylvan, yes, but almost
    dishonored by mere,

still, being? On my side, leaves against the
    glass and then, left frame, on the rooftop of some walled industrial
                                facility,
a mounted, scanning, video-cam—
    searching for what?—inside the walls then out—

(no windows there)—(below, a parking lot)—
    lens all one way, then back the
other way . . . *Where is,* I think,

     watching again,
the blind spot in its turn?
    Across the aisle (now lights are out) the sea's skin
gleams.
    Two clouds. Two evergreens.
My neighbors have gone back to sleep.
    When does it change—the frame around her scene,

the frame around my scene?
    After a while I see he's not her dad.
Then that they're stoned and cannot help the sleep.
    The sea that holds them in its frame—stuck there—
itself is stuck, slick gaping eyelessness.
    Where is the news account?
Where is the *varnished* sea? where the ventriloquial sea, the fast
                             train—panning

glints—scribble of shifting points of view—
    wave-tips frothing as the eye
blinks and the venue slips
    to the new sea—*of faces,* say, *of houses*—and then some
                       even newer
sea—hiding its monster? white-eyed? . . . I want it to be again
                 what it was—
    to go by and go by, as if matter itself were going

on and on to its own
    destination, bouquet of instances collecting all
the swift and cunning and mercenary
    appearances—swish—so that it's *there, there,*
and we can, swaying slightly,
    eyes still, eyes absolutely open receptive and still,
let it lay itself down frame by frame onto the wide

resistanceless opening of our wet
retina—more and more—
    all the debris, all the astonishments, quicker than single file,
smearing onto us—undestined, undestinied—
    But it is still. It does not move.

2

Against my pane,
    flat leaves that would bury themselves
into the molecules of glass—pressed
    right up to my eye—(so close they blur)—
the flat cold lingering
    against my skin

    as I pull back.
A scribble of only . . . Lowly . . . Green ribbon. They twitch (no
    wind). They peck a bit (now wind). A stratagem
                              for genuine
utterance—cunning, teasing the invisible tender-minded
                        spectrum
    of. . . . The cam keeps saying something about

sight—
    about the guaranteed freshness of the world repeating
                                  itself
without meaning—leaf, leaf—
    Shanavasa asked Ananda,
"what is the fundamental uncreated essence of all
    things?"
Come back come back with empty hands, he said,
    and
where can dust collect?
    (time and again wipe it diligently)
and
    there has never been anything

166

given to another, there has never been anything
received from another . . .
Look close, I think. Stem, node,
    bract, pedicel.
I count the greens.
    I slow along the veins.
And shadow: how it slithers long the rib: how it is seized,

fretted—shouldered here and slipped-off there—
    so that no two faces
match,
    each branch a sea of
individual
    tremblings—
I want to see through—my window does not open or

    I'd take a leaf—from here
(against the light) the chlorophyll exists inside the plasts
    and (where sun is strongest) light
thickens
    drawing the carbon
in . . .

    Oxygen steams off.
Sun picks up mist.
    Under the face of it I see the pores
between the veins.
    Where the carbon molecule must pass. Where the hydrogen
                          molecule
must pass.
    Inside, inside.
Envelope, rib, protein, thylakoid,
    starch grain,
acid strand.

And the cuticle of the leaf brim.
    And the loosely packed layer of photosynthetic tissue,

guard cells,
  substomatal chambers. . . .

  I blink. I don't *see anything.*
Lord,
  I want to see this leaf. I'd shut my hand all round it. I'd press it,
                                                            tight.

                              3

  What does she have, my twin, the sleeper, there, unseized,
in her window-sea?
  God's adversary: the waters?
Unfanged, unhanded, unlimbed, unheaded?
  Hooves and hooves and hooves and hooves?
The protozoa bloom all over its back.
  It hunches and slacks. Amasses and slacks.
All its passageways gleam.
  They breathe, the two of them.
They have a shopping bag on the floor between them—a large
                                    toy train

  in glistening packaging—red white and blue
and green and chrome.
  Thou didst divide the sea by thy strength: thou breakest
the heads of the dragons
  in the waters:
thou driest up the mighty river:
  the day is thine:
thou has prepared the light:
  thou has set all the borders of:
when the waves of the sea arise
  thou stillest them:
with thy strong arm:
  awake awake:
awake awake:
  thou has made over the deep of the sea a way

for the ransomed to pass over—

      Green leaves: cloth to shroud the Deep:
ride above the deep:
      ride in your chariot of shapeliness:
clean: shut: not this and not this:
      destroy with one seed the monster's skull:
thrust with one stem a sword into its heart—

      And the waters fled *backwards*—
And the endlessness fearfully surrendered—
      And the branching dried up the floods,
dividing,
      dividing,
and the minutes sang, each to each,
      and the minutes the sons of god shouted for joy, tick tock,

      thus the work of creation was
completed.
      And I see on her arms the needle-tracks.
His neck—long where it's tossed in sleep—has tracks.
      And the tops of her hands, folded, tracked.
She's wearing running shoes. She's shivering—

      asleep and shivering. Wouldn't you cover her
with the man-sized coat bunched up beside her,
      just take it gently—(like this)—holding my breath—
and pull it over her—(like this)—(as if to hide her)—
      but she will waken suddenly
and think I'm stealing it
      and scream
and will not listen where I'm trying to
      explain.
She hits my face.
      Making my right eye smart.
It's like a dream but it is not a dream.

What would you cover up?
    what, recover from His sight?
What, restore to the deep
    sleep and
why? *Whir.*
    We have been monitoring developments.
The first shells fell just a hundred yards from.
    Others were killed on the way to.
As the search for food becomes more difficult.
    Lost his legs on the way to.
Earlier the representative said.
    The People's Congress said.
The prime minister said.
    Lost his legs in the attack, up the front steps.

    Others were killed on the way to;
others were killed on the way too;
    and in a border-skirmish at dawn the parties involved pledged—
What is the fundamental uncreated essence of all
    things the representative
asked—
    Come back come back with empty hands the minister
pledged—In

    1982 on the downtown Express just out of 72nd Street,
having found a seat in what is like a dream, the sideways-rocking
    mixed-in with the forward
lunge making me slightly
    sleepy, watching the string of faces lined up across from
                    me—
the interlocking vertebrae
    of the endless twisting creature's spine—

    watching it lob to absorb the shocks—
watching it twist all one way to wreathe

            the rudderless turns—
watching the eyes in it narrow, widen, as the tunneling forwardness
        cleaved to its waiting like flesh—
widen and narrow—blinking—the whole length of the train (I thought)
        this dynamism of complex acceptance,
sleepy, staring out,
        blinking, some equation getting counted
out—change by change—sometimes the elbows touching, sometimes
                                        the seam at
        the thigh—plus or minus—some long bit of
thought—what needs to be under-
        gone that the solution be

found—sleepy—then
        an utterly single sound, sawtoothed, a fragment
of some vacuum, flew
        into the car and the woman beside me doubled
over and faster and faster the figures in the long
        equation began to twist and stand—a long distorted
sound—then a snapping into the present tense
        like surfacing and M grabbed me and pushed me
down, *down* he shrieked, and shoved me behind
        the last row of seats and the boy

waving the gun made a shape in the air above his head
        like a wave breaking upon a rock—
or was he giving up?—a shape in the invisible which expresses
        hope, then down came the arm again, and more
shots, and screams, the boy bending forward with his long
        extended arm as if

        trying to include something in himself,
as if trying to sharpen himself for entry,
        the room a brightly-lit hole hurtling through space at 90 mph,
a hole with screams and lights and bullets traveling round,
        holding the emptiness together—so that

171

it matters—
    light and blood swirling—us down here

on our knees in
    secret, living, living,
my portion of time,
    my portion, full,
(can you stand it?)
    (get down and hide)
(live fast, cloth over a sea, breathe, breathe)

    and at the heart of the living hole the boy, acid,
rare, in support of progress,
    looking for what he's missed,
laughing, gun at the end of his arm, over his
    head, swinging back,
tentacular, spitting seed, him the stalk of
    the day, scattering seed, planting it deep—

here and here—into everything he reaches,
    all things can happen,
wave after wave,
    seek and thou shall find,
and yet so unlikely,
    so that one is not sure of having seen—
wet branches? what was I wearing?
    and then much later, like a dream, desolate, things
                  being talked about.

172

IN THE HOTEL   (3:17 A.M.)

Whir. The invisible sponsored again by white
walls—a joining in them and then (dark spot)
(like the start of a thought)
a corner, fertilized by shadow, hooked, dotted,
here demurring, there—up there—
almost hot with black. . . . What time is it?
The annihilation. The chaste middle of things.
Then I hear them, whoever they are, as if
inside my wall, as if there were a multitude of tiny wings
                                        trapped
inside the studs and joints.
The clockdial hums. Greenish glow and twelve stark dots
round which this supple, sinewed, blackest flesh
must roil—vertebrate. A moaning now—a human moan—and then
another cry—but small—
furry in the way the wall can hold it—no
regret—a cry like an hypothesis—another
cry—the first again?—but not as in
dialogue—no—no question in it,
no having heard—now both—no moods in that room—
no fate—cries the precipitate of something on the verge of—
all of it supple now, threadbare in this black we share,
little yelps, vanquishings, discoveries, here under this
                                        rock,
no, over here, inside this sky, or is it below?—paupers,
                                        spoors—
a common grave—the backbone still glowing green—
and blackness, and the sense of walls, and the voicing they
provide, and my stillness here—unblinking—I am almost
                                        afraid
to move—and the litheness of this listening—
gossipy murmuring syllables now rushing up the scales,
but not really towards, not really away,
as if the thing deepened without increase,
the weight of the covers upon me,

the weight of the black, the slack, and heaving argument
                              of gravity—
and her quavering, lingering—
and him—what had been mossy
                  suddenly clawed—
and everything now trying to arrive on time, ten thousand
                              invisible things all
braided in, fast—*appetite, the clatter of wheels upon tracks,
the rustling—what did I lose?—what was it
like?*—the weight of covers now upon me like the world's
                                    shut lid,

shut fast—not opening—
and cries, and cries, and something that will not come true.
When I stand up, pulling the heavy bedclothes back,
I want to open up the black.
Water sounds in the pipes between us.
A raised voice. Some steps.
More water in the singing pipes.
And scuffling. And the clicking of their light going off . . .
Debris of silences inside the silence.
Black gorged with absences. Room like an eyelid
                        spanked open
wide, I rip it, I rip it further—as if inside it now the million
tiny slippages could go to work, the whistling
                        of absence
where the thing *should care for us*—
where justice shifts and reshifts the bits to make
                        tomorrow—
tirelessly—kingdom of scribble and linger. . . . What do you
want, *you*, listening here with me now? Inside the
                              monologue,
what would you insert? What word?
What mark upon the pleating blacknesses of hotel air?
What, to open it? To make it hear you. To make it hear me.
How heavy can the singleness become?
Who will hear us? What shall we do?
I have waited all this time in the sooty minutes,

174

green gleaming bouquet offering and offering itself
right to my unrelenting open eyes,
long black arm tendering its icy blossoms up to me,
right through the blizzard of instances, the blurry
blacknesses, the whole room choked with the thousand spots
                              my glance has struck—
Long ago, long ago, and then, second-hand, this place
                              which is now,
whir—immortal? free?—glances like flames licking the walls . . .
Oh blackness, I am your servant. I take for mine your green, exactest,
                                                            gift

in which you say yourself, in which you say
only yourself—

THE DREAM OF THE UNIFIED FIELD

1

On my way to bringing you the leotard
you forgot to include in your overnight bag,
the snow started coming down harder.
I watched each gathering of leafy flakes
melt round my footfall.
I looked up into it—late afternoon but bright.
Nothing true or false in itself. Just motion. Many strips of
motion. Filaments of falling marked by the tiny certainties
of flakes. Never blurring yet themselves a cloud. Me in it
                                             and yet
moving easily through it, black Lycra leotard balled into
                                     my pocket,
your tiny dream in it, my left hand on it or in it
                            to keep
warm. Praise this. Praise that. Flash a glance up and try
                                 to see
the arabesques and runnels, gathering and loosening, as they
define, as a voice would, the passaging through from
                              the-other-than-
human. Gone as they hit the earth. But embellishing.
Flourishing. The road with me on it going on through. In-
scribed with the present. As if it really
were possible to exist, and exist, never to be pulled back
in, given and given never to be received. The music
of the footfalls doesn't stop, doesn't
mean. *Here are your things,* I said.

2

Starting home I heard—bothering, lifting, then
                       bothering again—

176

the huge flock of starlings massed over our
                              neighborhood
these days; heard them lift and
swim overhead through the falling snow
as though the austerity of a true, cold thing, a verity,
the black bits of their thousands of bodies swarming
                              then settling
overhead. I stopped. All up and down the empty oak
they stilled. Every limb sprouting. Every leafy backlit
                              body
filling its part of the empty crown. I tried to count—
then tried to estimate—
but the leaves of this wet black tree at the heart of
                    the storm—shiny—
river through limbs, back onto limbs,
scatter, blow away, scatter, recollect—
undoing again and again the tree without it ever ceasing to be
                                        full.
Foliage of the tree of the world's waiting.
Of having waited a long time and
                    still having
to wait. Of trailing and screaming.
Of engulfed readjustments. Of blackness redisappearing
                              into
downdrafts of snow. Of indifference. Of indifferent
                    reappearings.
              I think of you
back of me now in the bright house of
                    your friend
twirling in the living room in the shiny leotard
                    you love.
I had looked—as I was leaving—through the window

to see you, slick in your magic,
pulling away from the wall—

I watch the head explode then recollect, explode, recollect.

3

Then I heard it, inside the swarm, the single cry

of the crow. One syllable—one—inside the screeching and the
                                                    skittering,
inside the constant repatterning of a thing not nervous yet
                                        not ever
still—but not uncertain—without obedience
yet not without law—one syllable—
black, shiny, twirling on its single stem,
rooting, one foot on the earth,
twisting and twisting—

and then again—a little further off this time—*down the
ravine,* voice inside a head, filling a head. . . .

See, my pocket is empty now. I let my hand
open and shut in there. I do it again. Two now, skull and
                                        pocket
with their terrified inhabitants.

       You turn the music up. The window nothing to you, liquid, dark,
where now your mother has come back to watch.

Closeup, he's blue—streaked iris blue, india-ink blue—and
black—an oily, fiery set of blacks—none of them
true—as where hate and order touch—something that cannot
become known. Stages of black but without
graduation. So there is no direction.
All of this happened, yes. Then disappeared
into the body of the crow, chorus of meanings,
layers of blacks, then just the crow, plain, big,

lifting his claws to walk thrustingly
forward and back—indigo, cyanine, beryl, grape, steel . . . Then suddenly he
wings and—braking as he lifts
the chest in which an eye-sized heart now beats—
—he's up—a blunt clean stroke—
one ink-streak on the early evening snowlit scene—
See the gesture of the painter?—Recall the
crow?—Place him quickly on his limb as he comes sheering in,
close to the trunk, to land—Is he now
disappeared again?

5

. . . . *long neck, up, up with the head,*
eyes on the fingertips, bent leg, shift of
the weight—*turn*—No, no, begin again . . .
What had she seen, Madame Sakaroff, at Stalingrad, now in
her room of mirrors tapping her cane
as the piano player begins the interrupted Minuet again
and we line up right foot extended, right
                        hand extended, the Bach mid-phrase—
Europe? The dream of Europe?—midwinter afternoon,
rain at the windowpane, ceilings at thirty feet and coffered
floating over the wide interior spaces . . .
No one must believe in God again I heard her say
one time when I had come to class too soon
and had been sent to change. The visitor had left,
kissing her hand, small bow, and I had seen her (from the curtain)
(having forgotten I was there)
turn from the huge pearl-inlaid doors she had just closed,
one hand still on the massive, gold, bird-headed knob,
and see—a hundred feet away—herself—a woman in black in
                        a mirrored room—
saw her not shift her gaze but bring her pallid tensile hand—
as if it were not part of her—slowly down from

the ridged, cold, feathered knob and, recollected, fixed upon

                                that other woman, emigrée,

begin to move in stiffly towards her . . . You out there

                                           now,

you in here with me—I watched the two of them,

black and black, in the gigantic light,

glide at each other, heads raised, necks long—

me wanting to cry out—where were the others?—wasn't it late?

the two of her like huge black hands—

clap once and once only and the signal is given—

but to what?—regarding what?—till closer-in I saw

                               more suddenly

how her eyes eyed themselves: no wavering:

like a vast silver page burning: the black hole

                            expanding:

like a meaning coming up quick from inside that page—

coming up quick to seize the reading face—

each face wanting the other to *take* it—

but where? and *from* where?—I was eight—

I saw the different weights of things,

saw the vivid performance of the present,

saw the light rippling almost shuddering where her body finally

                                  touched

the image, the silver film between them like something that would have

                                shed itself in nature now

but wouldn't, couldn't, here, on tight,

between, not thinning, not slipping off to let some

                              seed-down

through, no signal in it, no information . . . Child,

                       what should I know

to save you that I do not know, hands on this windowpane?—

                           6

The storm: I close my eyes and,

standing in it, try to make it *mine.* An inside

thing. Once I was. . . . once, once.
It settles, in my head, the wavering white
sleep, the instances—they stick, accrue,
grip up, connect, they do not melt,
I will not let them melt, they build, cloud and cloud,
I feel myself weak, I feel the thinking muscle-up—
outside, the talk-talk of the birds—outside,
strings and their roots, leaves inside the limbs,
in some spots the skin breaking—
but inside, no more exploding, no more smoldering, no more,
inside, a splinter colony, new world, possession
gripping down to form,
wilderness brought deep into my clearing,
out of the ooze of night,
limbed, shouldered, necked, visaged, the white—
now the clouds coming in (don't look up),
now the Age behind the clouds, The Great Heights,
all in there, reclining, eyes closed, huge,
centuries and centuries long and wide,
and underneath, barely attached but attached,
like a runner, my body, my tiny piece of
the century—minutes, houses going by—The Great
                                        Heights—
anchored by these footsteps, now and now,
the footstepping—now and now—carrying its vast
white sleeping geography—mapped—
not a lease—*possession*—"At the hour of vespers
in a sudden blinding snow,
they entered the harbor and he named it Puerto de

7

San Nicolas and at its entrance he imagined he
                                        could see
its beauty and goodness, *sand right up to the land
where you can put the side of a ship.* He thought
                                        he saw

Indians fleeing through the white before
the ship . . . As for him, he did not believe what his
                                            crew
told him, nor did he understand them well, nor they
him. In the white swirl, he placed a large cross
                              at the western side of
the harbor, on a conspicuous height,
as a sign that Your Highness claim the land as
Your own. After the cross was set up,
three sailors went into the bush (immediately erased
from sight by the fast snow) to see what kinds of
trees. They captured three very black Indian
women—one who was young and pretty.
The Admiral ordered her clothed and returned to
                                    her land
courteously. There her people told
that she had not wanted to leave the ship,
but wished to stay on it. The snow was wild.
Inside it, though, you could see
this woman was wearing a little piece of
gold on her nose, which was a sign there was
                        gold
on that land"—

MANIFEST DESTINY

*In the center of Georgiana's left cheek there was a singular mark, deeply interwoven, as
it were, with the texture and substance of her face. . . .*
(HAWTHORNE)

1
(Pink Palace Museum, Memphis)

She lifts the bullet out of the blazing case.
Here.
What can it harm?
Clock on the wall.
Ceiling-fan on.
Earlier it was

muzzleflash, dust. All round in the woods
voices and orders but you can't be sure whose.
Here's a sunken place by the road for
shelter, for the speechless
reload.

Tents that way or is it fog?
Or is it freedom?
A horse with his dead man
disappears.
The line is *where* that has to be maintained at all

cost?
Smoke clears and here's
a thousand peachtrees,
a massacre of blooms, or is it smoke?
The fire is let go, travels into the blossoming (not as fast
as you'd

think) enters a temple then a thigh.
        Carrying one body into the other.
She holds up the set of knives in their calfskin case.
        Behind her the diorama where the field surgeon's
sawing.
        There's the wax mouth held shut.
There's the scream inside—gold, round.
        Peachblossoms fall.
No chloroform so whiskey's

        used and sometimes—now lifting up out of the
incandescent case—the
        bullet we bend close
to see the
        bitemarks on—three dark impressions—whose footprints
on bottomland—
        whose 8,000 bodies, sticky with blossom, loosening into the wet
                                        field,
the still-living moving the more

        obedient bodies of the already-dead
up and down during the night,
        petals continuing to cover them.
Flashes of lightning showed hogs feeding on the dead says the
        captain who hears the wounded rebel under him say "oh
God what made You

        come down here to fight? we never
would have come up there."
        Look, he lives to write it down.
Here are the black words photographed and blown
        up wall-size behind
the guide.

        Do you think these words are still enough?
And the next thing and the next thing?
        Where is the mark that stays?
Where is what makes a mark

184

that stays?

    What's *real* slides through.

The body rots. The body won't hold it.

    Here's the next room and the *flight simulator.*

We the living run our arms along the grooves as we walk through.

    They are lifted and dropped.

Experience wingaction.

    I shut my eyes and try it

again.

    The museum hums round me.

Something else,

    something niggardly letting the walls stay up for now, hums,

something speechless and dense and stationary letting

    matter coalesce

in obstinate illustration—hums.

    Hear the theories come to cloak it—buzz.

Hear the deafness all over the trees, green.

    Hear his scream go into the light.

See how the light is untouched

    by the scream that

enters it.

    Dust motes.

Peachblossom-fall.

    Where shall the scream stick?

What shall it dent?

    Won't the deafness be cracked?

Won't the molecules be loosened?

    Are you listening? We need the scream to leave its mark

on the silky down of

    the petaled

light—

2
(Peach Orchard, Shiloh Battlefield)
(Mississippi River)

She's the scream he's the light.
They are playing, sort of, at Leda and Swan.

No, she's the *stream* he's the *blossomfall?*

Do you think these words are still enough?

Something out there on a spot in the middle of the
river.

Where the sun hits first and most directly.

Where there's a little gash on the waterfilm.

An indentation almost a cut his foothold.

Her a stream, yes, though not less a girl,
him the light become winged in its lower reaches,
almost biting the water there where it touches

or so the story goes—

him needing something he did not have,

(all round them the confused clickings of matter)—

the insects whining high, whining low . . .

He wants to go into her, he goes through.

Can't seem to find her: can't seem to find her.

The more he enters the more she disappears.

Can't seem to find her, can't seem to find her.

The insects whining high, and whining low.

The toothed light down hard on the sinewy scream.

She is asking for it he is not there.

He is promising forever she is not there.

Do I own you she says—

Yes, yes he is not there—

She is rising up as he descends then she
        is not
there then she
        is water beneath him, a river is flowing

he's clawing for foothold the river won't take his mark—

Where she eddies it's brighter for an instant—
Where the scream is, the light is broken for
                        the instant—
Where the light is brighter the scream is
                        the instant—
Where they thought they could marry—
In which they thought they could touch
                        each other—
The instant: they can't see it: a scent: in it
        the place something maybe took

place but what—

How can the scream rise up out of its grave of matter?
How can the light drop down out of its grave of thought?

How can they cross over and the difference between them swell with
existence?

Everything at the edges of everything else now rubbing,

making tiny sounds that add up to laughter,

something the breeze can lift and drop,

something that clots here and there and confirms our
fear,

(and the laughter which you might *think* is an angel
above them)

(a body whose ribs are the limits of everything)

(oh but we are *growing* now that there's a hurry, aren't we?)

(here where nothing is alive and vastly limbed and eyed)

(and the future spreads before us the back of its long
                                                        body)

For the first time since Homer . . . whispers his open book,
spine up to the light,

and *Naturalism was already outmoded when* . . .

and *by visible truth we mean the apprehension of* . . .

3

Beautiful natural blossoms . . .

        What is this she lifts and puts into my palm,
this leaden permanence—ash
        of a man's scream still

188

intact?
       Strange how heavy it is I think.
And here are the in-
       dentations—
I run my finger in them,
       little consequence, firmer than the cause.

       The war is gone. The reason gone. The body gone. Its
reason gone. The name the face the personal
       identity and yet here
is a pain that will not
       diminish . . .
I stand with my hand out in front of me.
       Someone lifts the thing slightly

then puts it back down.
       I'm looking for contagion. I'm watching the face

       of my friend as he tries to see
deeply the bitten bullet without
       lifting his hand to touch.
I watch his eyes focus.
       I watch him try to see what there is to
see.
       The russet cord behind him gleams.
The ceiling fan.
       The woman's voice.
The windows to the
       left and through it

       blossoms in rain.
Little mist,
       you take the sunlight and its frequency,
which is a color, in,
       you have these teeth which are molecules,
and in them there is
       a form of desire

which ascertains what color of the light
        will do, into which then the molecules must bite
down, taking the necessary
        nutrient—color? speed?—
into themselves and,
        altering, matter

make—white and silky by virtue of what they
        do not
apprehend—

What does this young man's bite into the world
        take—
what nutrient
        does his bite find,

        what grows, white and airy and almost invisible,
out of him
        as of this
feeding?
        Here is the young man's great-grandfather himself a young man
getting off the boat
        in James Town, 1754, with a sack of seeds.

This is a peach seed. It has come from Amsterdam.
        Before it was in a crate unloaded in Venice.
A new thing for the human mind—a peach.
        Found in Baghdad by another young man.
Tasted out of curiosity.
        Here the spring of 1762 and the first blossoms,

        then a good summer, not much war, then the first
fruit.
        Here the wife's face, he is handing her a fruit.
She puts the churn down a minute. The child is crying.
        Here, he says, try it. And her mouth

over the rough skin, the fire
 needing attention, the child
starting to scream.
 Here the mark on the surface of that

peach.
 Here the note she puts in her journal
that night.
 The words for it—that taste.
The season it stands at the heart of, that
 sweetness not entirely sweet.
A fruit part sunshine part water she writes.
 But what she's thinking is his face when he came into the room

holding it
 this morning. What was it
he held in his hand
 that his face
could not see
 could not hold?

OPULENCE

The self-brewing of the amaryllis rising before me.
Weeks of something's decomposing—like hearsay
growing—into this stringent self-analysis—
a tyranny of utter self-reflexiveness—
its nearness to the invisible a deep fissure
the days suck round as its frontiers trill, slur
—a settling-ever-upward and then,
                              now,
this utterly sound-free-though-tongued opening
where some immortal scale is screeched—
bits of *clench, jolt, fray* and *assuage*—
bits of *gnaw* and *pulse* and, even, *ruse*
—impregnable dribble—wingbeat at a speed
too slow to see—stepping out of the casing outstretched,
                              high-heeled—
something from underneath coaxing the packed buds up,
loosening their perfect fit—the smooth skin between them
                              striating then
beginning to wrinkle and fold
so as to loosen the tight dictation of the four inseparable polished
                              and bullioned
buds—color seeping-up till the icy green releases the sensation of
                              a set of reds
imprisoned in it, flushed, though not yet truly
visible—the green still starchy—clean—
till the four knots grow loose in their armor,
and the two dimensions of their perfect-fit fill out and a third,
                              shadow, seeps in
loosening and loosening,
and the envelope rips,
and the fringes slip off and begin to fray at their newly freed tips,
and the enameled, vaulting, perfectly braided
                              Immaculate
is jostled, unpacked—

192

the force, the phantom, now sending armloads up
into the exclamation,
and the skin marbles, and then, when I look again,
has already begun to speckle, then blush, then a solid un-
avoidable incarnadine,
the fourness of it now maneuvering, vitalized,
like antennae rearranging constantly,
the monologue reduced—or is it expanded—to
this chatter seeking all the bits of light,
the four of them craning this way then that according to
the time
of day, the drying wrinkled skirts of the casing
now folded-down beneath, formulaic,
the light wide-awake around it—or is it the eye—
yes yes yes yes says the mechanism of the underneath tick tock—
and no footprints to or from the place—
no footprints to or from—

THE VISIBLE WORLD

I dig my hands into the absolute. The surface
                              breaks
into shingled, grassed clusters; lifts.
If I press, pick-in with fingers, pluck,
I can unfold the loam. It is tender. It is a tender
maneuver, hands making and unmaking promises.
Diggers, forgetters. . . . A series of successive single instances . . .
Frames of reference moving . . .
The speed of light, down here, upthrown, in my hands:
bacteria, milky roots, pilgrimages of spores, deranged
                              and rippling
mosses. What heat is this in me
that would *thaw time,* making bits of instance
                              overlap
shovel by shovelful—my present a wind blowing through
                              this culture
slogged and clutched-firm with decisions, overridings,
                              opportunities
taken? . . . If I look carefully, there in my hand, if I
                              break it apart without
crumbling: husks, mossy beginnings and endings, ruffled
                              airy loambits,
and the greasy silks of clay crushing the pinerot
                              in . . .
Erasure. Tell me something and then take it back.
Bring this pellucid moment—here on this page now
                              as on this patch
of soil, my property—bring it up to the top and out
                              of
sequence. Make it dumb again—won't you?—what
                              would it
take? Leach the humidities out, the things that will
                              insist on
making meaning. Parch it. It isn't hard: just take this

                                            shovelful
and spread it out, deranged, a vertigo of single
                                        clots
in full sun and you can, easy, decivilize it, un–
                                    hinge it
from its plot. Upthrown like this, I think you can
                                        eventually
abstract it. Do you wish to?
Disentangled, it grows very very clear.
Even the mud, the sticky lemon-colored clay
hardens and then yields, crumbs.
I can't say what it is then, but the golden-headed
                                    hallucination,
mating, forgetting, speckling, inter-
                            locking,
will begin to be gone from it and then its glamorous
                                            veil of
echoes and muddy nostalgias will
be gone. If I touch the slender new rootings they show me
                                            how large I
am, look at these fingers—what a pilot—I touch, I press
                                        their slowest
electricity. . . . What speed is it at?
What speed am I at here, on my knees, as the sun traverses now
                                            and just begins
to touch my back. What speed where my fingers, under the
                                        dark oaks,
are suddenly touched, lit up—so white as they move, the ray for
                                            a moment
on them alone in the small wood.
White hands in the black-green glade,
opening the muddy cartoon of the present, taking the tiny roots
                                        of the moss
apart, hired hands, curiosity's small army, so white
                            in these greens—
make your revolution in the invisible temple,
make your temple in the invisible

revolution—I can't see the errands you run, hands gleaming

for this instant longer

like tinfoil at the bottom here of the tall

whispering oaks . . .

Listen, Boccioni the futurist says a galloping horse

has not four

legs (it has twenty)—and "at C there is no sequence

because there is no time"—and since

at lightspeed, etc. (everything is simultaneous): my hands

serrated with desires, shoved into these excavated

fates

—mauve, maroons, gutters of flecking golds—

my hands are living in myriad manifestations

of light. . . .

"All forms of imitation are to be despised."

"All subjects previously used must be discarded."

"At last we shall rush rapidly past objectiveness" . . .

Oh enslavement, will you take these hands

and hold them in

for a time longer? Tops of the oaks, do you see my tiny

golden hands

pushed, up to the wrists,

into the present? Star I can't see in daylight, young, light

and airy star—

I put the seed in. The beam moves on.

THE SURFACE

It has a hole in it. Not only where I
concentrate.
The river still ribboning, twisting up,
into its re-
arrangements, chill enlightenments, tight-knotted
quickenings
and loosenings—whispered messages dissolving
the messengers—
the river still glinting-up into its handfuls, heapings,
glassy
forgettings under the river of
my attention—
and the river of my attention laying itself down—
bending,
reassembling—over the quick leaving-offs and windy
obstacles—
and the surface rippling under the wind's attention—
rippling over the accumulations, the slowed-down drifting
permanences
of the cold
bed.
I say *iridescent* and I look down.
The leaves very still as they are carried.

ABOUT THE AUTHOR

JORIE GRAHAM is the author of eight collections of poetry. She lives in Cambridge, Massachusetts, and teaches at Harvard University.